Welsh Wit & Wisdom

An Anthology of Quotations

WELSH WIT & WISDOM

Aubrey Malone

First impression: 2006

Cover design: Sion Ilar

ISBN: 0 86243 863 2

Printed on acid-free and partly recycled paper
and published and bound in Wales by
Y Lolfa Cyf., Talybont, Ceredigion SY24 5AP
e-mail ylolfa@ylolfa.com
website www.ylolfa.com
tel 01970 832 304
fax 832 782

Contents

INTRODUCTION

Pick up any anthology of quotations and the Welsh element in it will probably not be much more than 1%. And, like as not, that 1% will be comprised of dour utterances of a generic and stereotyped nature. What little humour there is will be diluted by clichéd depictions of the country and its people.

In these pages I've tried to give a cross-section of voices and themes, with the emphasis on succinctness – not easy for a Welsh person.

The vexed question of what Welshness is also raises its head in a book like this, and the answer, of course, is: How long is a piece of string?

The book has been chaptered alphabetically, according to themes, not all of which exemplify wit and/or wisdom. 'Dentopedology', for example, is a collection of 'foot-in-mouth' blunders.

Aubrey Malone, 2006

It's easier to quote someone than to think for oneself.
You can quote me on that.

DANNIE ABSE

ABSURDITIES

In 1981, the government-based Alkali Inspectorate named a factory at Aberavon the country's smokiest factory. It made smokeless fuels.

PHILIP MASON

Wales should be proud of being the humblest country in the world.

VERNON WATKINS

We grew the biggest onions in South Wales. My mother peeled one in Cardiff once and there were people crying in Swansea.

MAX BOYCE

On Sunday 5 April 1998 following a courageous fight for life, Catherine Thomas, *née* Holder, surrounded by family, died at home – and she's bloody annoyed.

OBITUARY NOTICE *in a Cardiff newspaper*

I'm a virgin and I brought up all my children to be the same.

SHIRLEY BASSEY

Liz Taylor recently remarked that Richard Burton often considered returning to Oxford to become a simple don. This was said with great sincerity and a straight face. Which, since the lady was at the time wearing a stupefying wig made from the scalps of at least nine healthy Italians and a frock costing upwards of $5000, gave me a poignant vision of donnish simplicity.

CARRIE NYE

I was in the Intelligence Corps in the army in the desert. I was so short and my bum so near the ground it always wiped out my footprints. Nobody could ever find me.

HARRY SECOMBE

My feet are killing me. Every night, when I'm lying in bed, they get me round the throat.

TOMMY COOPER

I'm a pacifist – with an accent on the 'Fist'.

T GWYNN JONES

It may have been just going wide but nevertheless it was a great shot on target.

TERRY VENABLES

Be here at ten o'clock on Thursday morning. They're delivering the earthquake.

IVOR NOVELLO *to a colleague, during rehearsals for 'Careless Rapture'.*

Most dentists' chairs go up and down but the one I was on went backwards and forwards. I thought, 'This is unusual.' Then, the dentist said, 'Cooper, get out of the filing cabinet.'

TOMMY COOPER

I spent twenty years perfecting the use of the colon: and then the war came.

CHARLES MORGAN

Raich Carter even used to kick his own players in training.

JOHN CHARLES

Tommy Cooper did a great after-dinner speech once by just standing up. That's all he did. He just stood up and the place was in absolute hysterics. After several minutes of solid laughter, he turned round to his wife and said, 'I haven't said anything yet.' And the whole place went up again.

PAUL DANIELS

Peter Sellers could do every type of voice except his own. 'I don't know what I sound like,' he once said.

HARRY SECOMBE

I climbed a mountain and yelled, 'Hello!' A voice came back, saying, 'The echo is busy at the moment. Leave a message at the beep.'

EDDIE IZZARD

We had a topless lady ventriloquist in Liverpool once. Nobody ever saw her lips move.

KEN DODD

Being a millionaire is a lot like being poor, except that you have a lot of money.

GRIFF RHYS JONES

There's no way Ryan Giggs is another George Best. He's another Ryan Giggs.

DENIS LAW

This is how he directed us: 'Go down that road until you come to nothing at all and then turn left.'

SIAN PHILLIPS *after asking an Irishman for street directions one night when she was lost in London*

ACTORS AND ACTING

Acting isn't a real man's work. I should be down the mines like my da instead of mincing about a stage in poofter's clothes with slap all over my face.

RICHARD BURTON

My childhood movie hero was James Dean. I thought acting was just about looking miserable and scuffling around.

ANTHONY HOPKINS

Within this actor there is always something reserved, a secret upon which trespassers will be prosecuted, a rooted solitude, which his Welsh blood tinges with mystery.

KENNETH TYNAN *on Richard Burton*

There's something cool about being a vain egotistical actor.

IOAN GRUFFUDD

Orson Welles can write, direct and produce. And, perhaps even more surprisingly, even act.

RAY MILLAND

Blank face is fine. The art of acting is not to act. Once you show the audience too much, what you are in fact showing them is bad acting.

ANTHONY HOPKINS

Richard Burton is impossible to direct when he's drunk and only half there when he's sober. He's wooden as a board with his body, doing all his acting with his voice.

JOHN BOORMAN

Charles Laughton was the most vulgar actor of all. You always thought when you saw him, 'What a great performance,' or 'What a ridiculous performance.' It was brassy and extraordinary.

ANTHONY HOPKINS

I tried the church and that failed. I was too dim for accountancy, too short-sighted for the police force and an insufficient liar to make a good politician. What else was left but for me to become an actor?

DESMOND LLEWELLYN, *aka Q in the Bond movies*

His handling of crowds was fantastic but he didn't know a damn thing about acting.

RAY MILLAND *on Cecil B de Mille*

My headmaster once told me that all actors, by definition, were homosexuals and communists.

TERRY JONES

Sean Connery was always more interested in talking to the technicians than the other actors on any film we made together.

DESMOND LLEWELLYN

You see them in supermarkets, usually in curlers, pushing some brat in a shopping cart and looking as if they dressed out of a Goodwill truck. Their cry is that they're being honest, like the girl next door. But their honesty stops when they forget to mention that they're earning a couple of hundred thousand a year that they hang onto while their mother is probably mucking out a chicken coop somewhere in Nebraska,

RAY MILLAND *on actresses from the 'Realist' school*

In each case, I fell in love with the man, only to see him disappear into the actor.

ELIZABETH HARRISON *on her two husbands, Richard Harris and Rex Harrison*

I am not a highbrow, I am an entertainer. Empty seats and good opinions mean nothing to me.

IVOR NOVELLO

ADULATION

This extraordinary figure of our time, this siren, this goat-footed bard, this half-human visitor to our age from the hag-ridden magic and enchanted woods of Celtic antiquity.

JOHN MAYNARD KEYNES *on David Lloyd George*

The Seven Wonders today would include Birmingham Water Works and the Menai Bridge.

H V MORTON

Tom Jones is the only man who's ever come anywhere close to the way I sing. He has that ballsy feeling, that 'I'm gonna shove it up your ass' attitude.

ELVIS PRESLEY

Swansea would never win a beauty competition but its people are fortunate because they live within a stone's throw of a perfect paradise – the Gower peninsula.

H V MORTON

Ryan Giggs gives defenders twisted blood.

GARY PALLISTER

When I go home nowadays I get the sort of kindliness normally reserved for dead people.

NEIL KINNOCK *in 1996*

My hero is the Greek mathematician Archimedes who watched the bath water rise above his navel and then rushed out into the street naked screaming, 'I found it! I found it!' forgetting that everyone was staring at his genitals.

DANNIE ABSE

Whether a film is good or bad, Marlon Brando is always compulsive viewing like Peter Lorre or Sydney Greenstreet. He's the greatest vulgarian of all time.

ANTHONY HOPKINS

Boy, wouldn't thirty million women like to be where I am now.

PRISCILLA PRESLEY, *while lying on a beach between Elvis Presley and Tom Jones*

I was always relieved to see him walk through the door to after-match dinners rather than just materialise through the wall.

GERALD DAVIES *on his rugby team-mate Barry John*

ADVICE

Never get mixed up in a Welsh wrangle. It doesn't end in blows like an Irish one, but goes on forever.

EVELYN WAUGH

Live large, man, and dream small.

R S THOMAS

If it should ever be your misfortune to have to spend Sunday in Wales, always get to windward when the chapels are disgorging the faithful.

ARTHUR JOHNSON

Quit playing wet nurse to an overgrown baby who'll destroy every last thing he can get his hands on, including himself.

TRUMAN CAPOTE *to John Malcolm Brinnin, whom he found excessively protective of Dylan Thomas*

Do not cry out against your native land for she will give you the two most exquisite pleasures of your life: that of leaving her and that of coming back.

DANNIE ABSE

The advice of a wife is worthless but woe to the man who doesn't take it.

OLD WELSH PROVERB

Learn to live on the knife edge of insanity.

SAUNDERS LEWIS

The best way to make your love life work is to make changes. Start with the locks on the front door.

KEITH BARRETT

AGE AND AGEING

After the age of eighty everything reminds you of something else.

LOWELL THOMAS

I am just turning forty – and taking my time about it.

HAROLD LLOYD *at 77*

When it comes to age, I'm a great believer in Maurice Chevalier's remark, 'There's only one difference between a man of 60 and a man of 40 – 20 years experience.'

ROY NOBLE

A compound Welsh dream would include Home Rule, Lloyd George's second coming, the declaration of a public holiday every time Wales score more than twenty points, and the compulsory retirement of committee chairmen after forty years in the chair, or on their hundredth birthday, whichever is sooner.

TREVOR FISHLOCK

Welsh romanticism has a startling arrogance. Ideally, it likes its heroes to die young. The dream is of the golden boy of natural genius who effortlessly conquers the English world. The romance lies in the ascent. Early death is attractive because it rules out the chances of solid middle age. The Welsh have all the talents, except for being 45.

JOHN MORGAN

I get increasingly disenchanted with acting. As the years totter past I find it ludicrous learning some idiot's lines in the small hours of the night so that I can stay a millionaire.

RICHARD BURTON

I'm the wrinklies' favourite these days.

RYAN GIGGS *at 28 in 2002*

Every man is an exile after the age of forty.

W J GRUFFYDD

I wish you could start having children when you're sixty.

DAWN FRENCH

A woman told her doctor, 'I've got a bad back.' The doctor said, 'It's old age'. The woman said, 'I want a second opinion'. The doctor said, 'Okay, you're ugly as well!'

TOMMY COOPER

I still want to be surprising people when I'm in my fifties.

RACHEL GRIFFITHS

You can tell the age of an individual not by inspecting their teeth but rather by how loudly they slam the front door shut.

DANNIE ABSE

1'm 27 years old and yet the referee tells me I'm not allowed to swear.

VINNIE JONES *in 1992, after being sent off for abusive language*

There's a deep anarchy in old age.

TERRY JONES

Whatever a man does after the age of forty should be forgiven because in nine cases out of ten he is utterly worn out by what has gone on before.

GWYN THOMAS

Today I am constantly forgetting what happened yesterday but things that happened 70 or 80 years ago are becoming much clearer.

AELWYN ROBERTS

Only grandfathers remember me now.

JOHN CHARLES IN 2003

How could I have an IQ of 25 when I'm only 23?

HELEN ADAMS *from* Big Brother 2

AGGRESSION

A man who deliberately uses words that others are likely to be ignorant of is committing a minor act of aggression.
> **DANNIE ABSE**

The Welsh aren't victims of English aggression. They're victims of Welsh aggression. The English were clever enough to let them get on with it.
> **JOHN RICHARDS**

I like to upset anybody I play against.
> **VINNIE JONES**

Go to take a corner at Elland Road and you've got 15,000 horrible skinheads yelling murder at you.
> **RYAN GIGGS**

We've got to be seen to be getting our retaliation in first.
> **NUM OFFICIAL** *during the miners' strike in 1985*

Just because he's world champion doesn't entitle him to be a cunt.
> **TERRY GRIFFITHS** *on Steve Davis, after he was late for an engagement. He later apologised and the pair became friends*

If I get near you once I'm going to rip your head off and crap in the hole.
> **VINNIE JONES** *to Kenny Dalglish after Dalglish fouled him in a match once*

A thwarted woman is a bear in the house.
> **RHYS DAVIES**

ALCOHOL

At last God caught his eye.

HARRY SECOMBE's *suggested epitaph for a barman*

When an Englishman has a pint too many he wants to fight or make love, or subside into the womb of smutty anecdote. When the Welshman stands behind the bar, he wants to sing.

JAMES MORRIS

A drunken man in a Swansea bar was going on and on. 'Did you know I can imitate any bird you care to mention?' he said. 'How about a homing pigeon?' said Gwladys, the barmaid.

WYNFORD JONES

If the eisteddfod is supposed to be alcohol-free, how is it that all the double-glazing reps are boozing it up in the hospitality areas behind the stands?

GREN JONES

There were once so many pubs in Llantrisant the church had a cork spire.

GWYN THOMAS

To speak English and get drunk were the insignia of a gentleman in the Wales that was.

REES EVANS

After I made *The Lost Weekend*, I found myself being looked upon as an authority on alcoholism. Me, for Christ's sake, a guy who had to be carted off to bed and given up for dead if he took three drinks!

RAY MILLAND

The nearest thing the Welsh have to a continental beer festival is The Rugby Trip. As a logistical exercise, preparation for this puts D-Day in the shade. The test of its success or failure is how much of it you can remember. If the whole weekend is a blank, then you must have enjoyed yourself.

JOHN RICHARDS

A Welshman doesn't need a reason to drink. All he needs is a drink.

GLYN ROBERTS

Teetotallers lack the sympathy and generosity of men that drink.

W H DAVIES

The main difference between League and Union rugby is that now I get my hangovers on Monday instead of Sunday.

TOM DAVID

I drink to make people bearable.

RICHARD BURTON

He would disappear for a quiet drink before dinner and not return for several weeks.

ELIZABETH HARRISON *on her former husband Richard Harris*

You can get high smoking pot and never get sick but it takes a man to be able to hold his liquor – and pay the penalty.

TOM JONES

If you drink whiskey straight down you can feel it going into each individual intestine.

RICHARD BURTON

I don't actually like alcohol. The only reason I drink is to get pissed and dance like a crazy woman.

CHARLOTTE CHURCH

Give real pain to your sham friends and champagne to your real friends.

BRYN ELLIS

I crossed to the drinks tray and picked up a soda siphon, turned it on him and put out the fire on his head.

SIAN PHILLIPS *on the Irish actor Donal McCann who set his hair on fire one night after falling into a drunken sleep with a cigarette in his hand.*

Jim Morrison was like a spoilt, clean-scrubbed schoolboy in his first day on drink.

JOHN CALE

The heavy drinker is simply fond of more, more and more drink. He it was who devised cunning schemes to bridge the gap between licensing hours with afternoon or all-night clubs, Turkish baths, Thames river trips and so on. It is surprising how many of my circle claimed at seven in the morning to have become overnight *bona fide* Covent Garden porters.

DAN JONES

I can get drunk on green tea.

AUGUSTUS JOHN

ANEURIN BEVAN INSULTS

Winston Churchill is a man suffering from petrified adolescence.

Listening to a speech by Neville Chamberlain is like paying a visit to Woolworth's: everything in its place and nothing above sixpence.

Clement Atlee seems determined to make a trumpet sound like a tin whistle.

Neville Chamberlain has all the lucidity of the sterile mind.

Walter Citrine, poor fellow, suffers from piles.

I have never regarded politics as an arena of morals. It is an arena of interests.

Churchill uses the majesty of his language to conceal the mediocrity of his thinking.

Walter Elliot is a man walking backwards with his face to the future.

The Tories always hold the view that the State is an apparatus for the protection of the swag of the property owners. Christ drove the moneylenders out of the temple, but they inscribe their title deeds on the altar cloth.

Clement Atlee brings to the fierce struggle of politics the tepid enthusiasm of a lazy summer afternoon at a cricket match.

Herbert Morrison is a squalid, backstairs, third rate Tammany Hall politician.

ANIMALS

A Welshman's horse is always descended from the beast ridden by Llewellyn the Great.

RHYS DAVIES

Only two things can save a cornered hare: God and a Cardiganshire jury.

TRADITIONAL SAYING

I used to know this dog that sat in front of the television set when there was rugby on. Every time Wales beat England at Cardiff Arms Park he used to jump up in the air and bark out the score. Frank Bough got to hear of him and came down to do a report. 'What does he do when England win?' He asked the owner. 'I don't know,' he replied, 'we've only had him fourteen years.'

MAX BOYCE

I always order Welsh lamb in restaurants in the hope that I'll get the woolly bastard that keeps tipping my dustbin over.

DINER *in a restaurant to Trevor Fishlock*

I christened my dog Hyphen-Jones on account of the Welsh aristocracy always calling themselves Something-Jones.

DESMOND LLEWELLYN

I can't work with horses in films. They're nightmares on four legs.

ANTHONY HOPKINS

A man in love makes a practical cat laugh.

DYLAN THOMAS

It isn't enough to have the eyes of a gazelle to paint properly. You also need the claws of a cat in order to capture your bird alive and play with it before you eat it and join its life to yours.

AUGUSTUS JOHN

The whole dilemma of living is summed up in the differing view of cats held by mice and lonely old ladies.

GWYN THOMAS

When you've been too long in the desert, a Newcastle lad said to me once, you start looking at the camels and thinking, 'Haven't they got nice long eyelashes?'

MAX BOYCE

To err is human, to moo bovine.

GWEN INGLIS

Western civilisation has gone from reality in the Middle ages, when humans merely stroked a dog, to the Renaissance, where we drew dogs, to modern times, when, under the influence of a drug, we see a fourteen-foot purple dog.

RICHARD BOOTH

APPEARANCE

I passed Nelson's column the other day. He was still checking to see if he had his ticket.

MAX BOYCE

The first time I saw Dylan Thomas I felt as if Rubens had suddenly taken it into his head to paint a youthful Silenus.

EDITH SITWELL

The population of Wales is two million or thereabouts, and the Welsh poets, male and female, but chiefly male, with flowing beards, would appear to include quite a million and a half.

T W CROSLAND

My nose has been broken so many times in punch-ups I can't remember which particular one made it this shape.

TOM JONES

I have a lot of sympathy with William Hague. I too was once a young, bald leader of the Opposition.

NEIL KINNOCK *in 1999*

Dorothy Kilgallen had no chin, Louella Parsons had no neck and Hedda Hopper had to wear strange hats to stand out in a crowd. I don't believe most of the men columnists were failed actors but most of the women gossips took out their frustrations on the beautiful actresses who became stars. They wrote with green ink.

RAY MILLAND

Not only did I have unfashionable beige hair, horrible National Health pink spectacles, big sticking-out front teeth and the longest, thinnest legs at school, I also had a flat chest.

JANET STREET-PORTER

Mark Hughes is playing better and better, even if he's going grey and starting to look like a pigeon.

GIANLUCA VIALLI IN 1997

If I'd had a face like Elizabeth Taylor I'd never have won two Oscars.

BETTE DAVIS

An incipient double chin, legs too short, and she has a slight pot belly.

RICHARD BURTON *on Taylor*

When I was born my mother said I looked like a frog.

CATHERINE ZETA-JONES

His face was his misfortune. Ivor was tripped up by his beauty.

PHYLLIS BOTTOME *on Ivor Novello*

When one has got used to wearing brilliant shirts and being stared at, all feeling of glamour fades away. But the mud, sweat and bumps are left.

DICK FRANCIS *on the gritty reality of being a jockey*

I think you'd better come at once, doctor. I don't like the look of my wife.

JOHN EDWARDS, *quoting an unfortunate turn of phrase used by an acquaintance on the phone*

Her face was too natural for the Fifties. She wasn't glossy and candy-box. One of nature's non-starlets.

HUNTER DAVIES *on Rachel Roberts*

Richard Harris makes me look sober.

RICHARD BURTON

Caitlin Thomas would strip at the drop of a hat. I would have too if I'd had her figure.

GWEN WATKINS

I have a face that looks like an unmade bed.

DYLAN THOMAS

After I got to Italy they told me I looked like a cross between Adolf Hitler and Charlie Chaplin.

IAN RUSH

If bees knew how good they looked in colour they would work through an agent.

GWYN THOMAS

BIRTH

Megan: 'I hear you is having triplets.'
Bethan: 'Yes, that's right.'
Megan: 'Duw, duw! That's amazing.'
Bethan: 'Yes, the doctor says it only happens once in two million times.'
Megan: 'Good grief. When did you have time to do the dishes?

WYNFORD JONES

Child-bearing is hereditary. If your parents didn't have any children, the chances are you won't either.

DICK CAVETT

I was born in Cardiff but at the age of six months I was persuaded by my parents to leave Wales.

GRIFF RHYS-JONES

My mother always says I hit the ground running.

IAN WOOSNAM

My arrival in this world attracted scant notice.

MICHAEL HESELTINE

Sian was going under the chloroform and the doctor, who had once played rugby for Ireland, was pulling the baby out. Sian suddenly started singing the unofficial Welsh anthem. The poor doctor – having played against Wales, where this thing is sung all the time at every game – felt as though he was in a rugby match, pulling a ball out of a scrum. Wasn't this a marvellous unconscious protest against being in Ireland?

PETER O'TOOLE *on his then wife Sian Phillips giving birth in Ireland*

I was born on the eighteenth of October 1943. It seems that I arrived soon after dinner. Mam timed it well. She loved her food.

DAI JONES

My wife only had seven children because she heard that every eighth child born in the world is Chinese.

GWYNFOR EVANS

I was born in the real world, not with a silver spoon in my mouth. If you plant a rose in the best soil it'll grow whatever you do. It's a lot harder growing in concrete.

VINNIE JONES

I was born in sorry circumstances. Both of my parents were very sorry.

STAN STENNETT

We're born in other people's pain and perish in our own.

DYLAN THOMAS

BOOKS

The National Library of Wales has four million books. They say it's the town with the highest ratio of books to people in the world. The problem was that, in order to become a reader, you needed to be vouched for by a respectable member of society, and that tended to eliminate most people in Aberystwyth.

MALCOLM PRYCE

When something new arrives in literature in Wales it is stamped upon at first and then imitated to death.

T GWYNN JONES

When Richard Llewellyn threw his atom bomb *How Green Was My Valley* into the world of letters, it shattered an ancient prejudice – that no novel about Wales could be financially successful.

WYN GRIFFITH

I read *The Happy Hooker* with dark glasses because I'm a Methodist.

MAIR GRIFFITHS

There are 40,000 children's books printed in Britain every year. Most of them are bloody awful, pulped and never reprinted.

ROALD DAHL

I once had a pastoral phase and slaved over a novel with the throat-slitting title *Nourished in the Grass*, which was intended as my answer to *How Green Was My Valley*. Unfortunately, a bucolic tale of life in the Lincolnshire fens was about as exciting as a sackful of dead mice.

BRYAN FORBES

My mother forbade me to read *Forever Amber*, so I read it in secret. There were also bits of *Antony and Cleopatra* that she wished she hadn't let me read. I wondered why she'd forgotten what a racy read the Old Testament was.

SIAN PHILLIPS

Books write authors as much as authors write books.

DICK FRANCIS

BORES

I am as keen as anyone on the due preservation of the Welsh language, but many fanatics are dancing around it like a lot of old-time Cherokee Indians round a totem-pole.

LORD OGMORE

The person who makes a bad thirty-minute speech to 200 people wastes only half an hour of his own time, but 100 hours of the audience's. That's more than four days. It should be a hanging offence.

JENKIN LLOYD JONES

Someone's boring me and I think it's me.

DYLAN THOMAS

Sexual inequality in the hands of ruthless employers is an abominable fraud, and in the mouths of the Women's Liberationists an absolute bore.

GWYN THOMAS

Neil Kinnock's speeches go on for so long because he has nothing to say so he has no way of knowing when he's finished saying it.

JOHN MAJOR

My worst fear is being sober and boring the piss out of everyone. Without alcohol I feel I belong in a university town somewhere, teaching literature and drama to grubby little boys.

RICHARD BURTON

Dullness in accountancy is considered an advantage.

TERRY JONES

The only thing a big band can do is mess around. Let's throw a spanner in the works. The thing about being established is that people get very boring. You have to invent challenges.

U2's *Edge*

Boredom is a vital problem for the moralist since half the sins of mankind are caused by fear of it.

BERTRAND RUSSELL

CAMARADERIE

To live in a town in West Wales is to know more people, and to know more about them than you ever will again, because this is the noisiest and most censorious society on earth. If you stole a wheelbarrow the whole town would know.

BYRON ROGERS

Don't ask me about emotion in a Welsh dressing-room. I cry when I watch *Little House on the Prairie*.

BOB NORSTER

An International at Twickenham is more than mere spectacle. It's the gathering of the clan.

JOHN MORGAN

Outside religious sects there has never been a closer community than that of the Welsh valleys.

BYRON ROGERS

CHAPELS

If people knew how much ill-feeling unselfishness occasions it would not be recommended so often from the pulpit.

C S LEWIS

Church-going declines not so much because of unbelief but because Dad has made a down-payment on the car.

ALAN JONES

The preacher's sermons were like water to a drowning man.

SELWYN V LEWIS

A lingerie factory, furniture showrooms, a strip-club, agriculture feed stores, bingo halls, recording studios, a boxing club, climbing centres, a Woman's Institute, the headquarters of the Welsh National Opera, and mosques.

ANTHONY JONES *after being asked what disused chapels were being turned into*

The chapels of Wales are closing at the rate of one a week. By the year 2000 the townscape of an entire country will be dominated by blackened teeth as, boarded up and abandoned, the chapels stampede out of history.

BYRON ROGERS *in 1988*

Poets are dangerous men to have in chapel.

IDRIS DAVIES

A chapel without women in it is as a summer dell without singing birds.

RHYS DAVIES

Wales would be brighter and more Christian-like if every chapel were burnt to the ground and a public house raised on the ashes thereof.

CARADOC EVANS

Welsh chapels are a depleted force. Preachers today aren't as athletic as they were in the old days, and some veteran chapel-goers hanker for the era of brimstone sermons of those who used the pulpit like a boxing ring as they fought to get the devil on the ropes.

TREVOR FISHLOCK

Welshmen in their chapels do not kneel in prayer. They bend down, sitting as though they are vomiting.

SAUNDERS LEWIS

The chapel preachers never lead the people except at funerals.

WILLIAM PRICE

I used to wonder why we never had any actors in Wales. Then I realised they all went into the pulpit, the greatest stage in the world. The chapel dominated every village. You stood, hovering like a great bird of prey over the people, and said, 'Let me examine your soul.'

RICHARD BURTON

CHILDHOOD AND CHILDREN

We bring up our children to speak Welsh not for the sake of the language but for the sake of our children.

IOAN BOWEN REES

We even played cowboys and Indians in Welsh.

AELWYN ROBERTS

There was a tremendous rumbling sound and all the school went dead. You could hear a pin drop. Everyone just froze in their seats. I managed to get up. I reached the end of my desk. When the sound got louder and nearer, I could see the black outside the window. I can't remember any more, but I woke up to find that a horrible nightmare had just begun in front of my eyes.

GAYNOR MINETT *on the 1966 disaster which claimed 144 lives in the mining village of Aberfan in South Wales after a waste tip slid down a mountainside engulfing everyone beneath it*

When I played rugby as a child we used kidney bean sticks for the goalposts and Fairy Liquid bottles for the ball. I was the best kicker of a Fairy Liquid bottle in all Glamorgan. I could screw kick to touch and make the top come off.

MAX BOYCE

I learned to ride when I was five, on a donkey.

DICK FRANCIS

I can never remember whether it snowed for six days and six nights when I was twelve, or whether it snowed for twelve days and twelve nights when I was six.

DYLAN THOMAS

They asked Jack Benny if he would do something for the Actors' Orphanage so he shot both his parents and moved in.

BOB HOPE

When I was young I was able to hypnotise people by pulling their ear lobes.

ANTHONY HOPKINS

If my father was the head of the house, my mother was its heart.

RICHARD LLEWELLYN

I was five years old when my mother told me I had a lovely voice. I was singing a song called 'Maizy Doats and Dozy Doats'. After that, there was no stopping me.

TOM JONES

The most embarrassing moment of my childhood was when I wet my knickers at the age of four. I had a jam jar full of water in my hand when it happened. I spilled the water all over the floor so you couldn't see the puddle I made.

CAROL VORDERMAN

Christmas was much more enchanting when I was a child. There were no bleary-eyed Santa Clauses on every street corner, begging for some charity or another, 90% of which you'd never heard of, each one of them ringing those damn bells.

RAY MILLAND

I didn't have many luxuries as a child. I got my first pair of boots when I was six. Two of my brothers had worn them before me. They were probably older than I was.

IAN RUSH

The smell of wet knickers, orange peel and carbolic acid flowed over us like a warm, sticky bath.

HARRY SECOMBE *remembering the cinema he attended as a child*

Who has not watched a mother stroke her child's cheek or kiss her child in a certain way and not felt a nervous shudder at the possessive outrage done to a free solitary human soul?

JOHN COWPER POWYS

I've been camp since I was about seven.

DAVID BOWIE

I was a boy from a 'means-test' family. I was dressed in the uniform of the poor. I had no hair. My head was shaved like a convict, with just a fringe at the front. I used to always wear a grey jersey made of steel wool, patched trousers that were patched again each time I tore them, and bloody great boots, great clodhoppers, always sizes too big, so they'd last a long time.

STANLEY BAKER

In my childhood a belief in the unity and brotherhood of man was as urgent and compelling a force as the gambling mania of today. We lifted our eyes unto the hills with such dedication the hills got jumpy.

GWYN THOMAS

I grew up in Europe, where the history comes from.

EDDIE IZZARD

One day my father came running into the room, waving a £5 note and saying, 'Look what I've got for you, son.' He'd sold me.

KEN DODD

CLOTHING

It takes forty dumb animals to make a fur coat but only one to wear it.

BRYN JONES

If you had boots as a kid rather than shoes you were definitely inferior where I came from. It was like your mother having to buy margarine instead of butter.

STANLEY BAKER

I'm a clothesaholic.

CHARLOTTE CHURCH

I don't wear denims any more for the same reason Elton John doesn't wear platform heels or Rod Stewart doesn't wear leotards. They're too retro.

SHAKIN' STEVENS

I'd like to think I would put a coat down in a puddle for a lady. Depends how much I paid for it, I guess.

IOAN GRUFFUDD *on chivalry*

It's not easy to swordfight when you're wearing a corset and petticoats.

CATHERINE ZETA-JONES *on making* The Legend of Zorro

A national newspaper blamed the breakdown of my marriage on a blue dress I once wore!

CAROL VORDERMAN

COMPARISONS

Having a debate on the National Health Service without Aneurin Bevan is like putting on *Hamlet* with no one in the part of the First Gravedigger.

IAN MACLEOD

Lloyd George would have had a better rating in British mythology if he had shared the fate of Abraham Lincoln.

JOHN GRIGG

Swansea has got as many layers as an onion, and each one reduces you to tears.

DYLAN THOMAS

In Cardiff they'll talk about 'going to a paaatee'. The first part of the word is like the sound a person would make when falling off a cliff – 'aaagh'.

MICHAEL ASPEL

Learning Welsh is a lot like jumping off the bridge of common sense.

PAMELA PETRO

I once made an effort to master elephant polo in Delhi. It was a bit like playing golf with a fishing rod.

MAX BOYCE

He has a neck built like a stately home staircase.

TOM DAVIES *on boxer John Conteh*

He looks like he's making love to fresh air.

GORDON MILLS *on Tom Jones' pelvic gyrations on stage*

Having starred with Clint Eastwood, I cannot quite say it was a thespic experience on the order of Lunt and Fontaine acting together.

RICHARD BURTON

Steve Davis and Stephen Hendry play a different kind of snooker. Davis strangles you slowly.

TERRY GRIFFITHS

I made more farewell appearances than Frank Sinatra.

IAN RUSH

My memory of his books tangles with my memory of Henry Lamb's marvellous portrait of an outraged wet mackerel of a man, dropped like an old cloak into a basket chair.

T E LAWRENCE *on Lytton Strachey*

Vinnie Jones is as discreet as a scream in a cathedral.

FRANK MCGHEE

Duncan Mackenzie is like a beautiful motor car – six owners, but he's been in the garage most of the time.

JOHN TOSHACK *in 1978*

Coffee in England always tastes like a chemistry experiment.

AGATHA CHRISTIE

He was as alone as an old maid in a highland croft.

EMLYN WILLIAMS

Being attacked by Geoffrey Howe in the House is a bit like being savaged by a dead sheep.

DENIS HEALEY

It's like watching your mother-in-law drive off a cliff in your new car.

> **TERRY VENABLES** *on Paul Gascoigne's departure from Spurs in 1992*

He had eyebrows like handlebar grips.

> **MELVYN BRAGG** *on Hugh Griffith*

For some people, getting into trouble is a skill, like throwing darts or playing the banjo.

> **GWYN THOMAS**

It was like a marriage, except we got on better than most couples.

> **CAROL VORDERMAN** *on her relationship with Richard 'Countdown' Whiteley.*

Trevor Ford used to collect bookings like autographs.

> **JOHN CHARLES**

The best way to describe it is to imagine putting a cricket pitch in there. Bowl off a three yard run and you could still have wicket-keeper and slips standing back.

> **BARRY JOHN** *on the penthouse of Stanley Baker on the Thames*

DEATH

To live in Wales is to know that the dead outnumber the living.

> **DUNCAN BUSH**

Sign in a Welsh cemetery: 'Due to industrial go-slow difficulties, grave-digging this week will be done by a skeleton crew.'

> **GORDON IRVING**

I would die for my country but I could never let my country die for me.

NEIL KINNOCK *on the dangers of nuclear war*

Here lies Harry Secombe until further notice.

SECOMBE's *suggestion for his headstone*

Death is the most convenient time to tax rich people.

DAVID LLOYD GEORGE

In my experience of funerals in Wales, everybody wants something. Death is a great time for grabbing the leftovers.

ALUN OWEN

No matter how shabbily you've lived, you will be respected in Wales when you have become a corpse.

EDWARD VALE

Overheard at a seance in Boncath: 'Is there anybody there? Knock once for Yes and twice for No.'

WYNFORD JONES

I once attended a funeral on the day Wales lost an important match against England. It totally spoiled the day for me.

DAI JENKINS

Speaking Welsh is the poor man's way of flirting with immortality.

PAMELA PETRO

I hope you die before me because I don't want you singing at my funeral.

SPIKE MILLIGAN *to Harry Secombe*

Maybe James Dean is lucky he died when he did. I saw *East of Eden* the other night. His performance is so stereotyped. All the bad imitations have destroyed him.

ANTHONY HOPKINS

My wife told me I'd drive her to the grave. I had the car out in two minutes.

TOMMY COOPER

Many men would take a death sentence without a whimper to escape the life sentence fate carries in her other hand.

T E LAWRENCE

The theme of death is to poetry what mistaken identity is to drama.

DANNIE ABSE

Most Welsh people have an almost morbid fascination with the subject of death. Many will let themselves go short of necessities in their old age in order to save money for a good funeral, thereby probably hastening the day.

JOHN RICHARDS

You never get to be a great actor until you're dead.

RICHARD BURTON

Both love and fear of death co-exist in most men.

DAN JONES

Everyone, even the police, said what a ghastly man the judge was. He died soon afterwards, so we were all rather pleased.

MAIDIE ANDREWS *on the prison sentence Ivor Novello received in 1944 after being convicted of a motoring offence*

Although it may seem that steeplechase jockeys are recklessly risking their lives in a dangerous sport, it is a matter of record that the death rate of window cleaners is very much higher. If any window cleaners' wives are reading this, I sincerely apologise for passing on that most unwelcome piece of news.

DICK FRANCIS

In Germany democracy died by the herdsman's axe. In Britain it can be by pernicious anaemia.

ANEURIN BEVAN

We are all afraid of death because we are all doing it for the first time.

GWEN DAVIES

Newton should have stayed in the orchard a little longer and deduced a law about the gravitational pull that death and ruin exercise on the human will.

GWYN THOMAS

I should like to make an enchanting curtain speech at the end of a wildly successful first night and, to the sound of cheers and applause, drop gracefully dead. Before the curtain falls, if possible.

IVOR NOVELLO

I became mortal the night my father died.

DANNIE ABSE

DEFINITIONS

Cardiff is the settled Zion of the Welsh Israelites.

GWYN THOMAS

Envy is the basis of democracy.
BERTRAND RUSSELL

A bucket of cold water and a sponge.
JOHN CHARLES *on the state of soccer physiotherapy in England in the 1950s*

The Welsh are the Jews of Britain.
ERNEST JONES

An actor is something less than a man. An actress is something more than a woman.
RICHARD BURTON

The enemy of idealism is zealotry.
NEIL KINNOCK

Ferdinand Foch is just a frantic pair of moustaches.
T E LAWRENCE

A tourist is someone who travels 3,000 miles to have himself photographed in front of his car.
ROBERT BENCHLEY

A house is only something to put around you to keep the weather out.
DYLAN THOMAS

Politics is a blood sport.
ANEURIN BEVAN

Richard [Burton] is the Frank Sinatra of Shakespeare.
LIZ TAYLOR

A cult figure is a guy who hasn't got the musical ability to make it into the charts.

JOHN CALE

Autobiography is the height of egoism.

ROALD DAHL

Love is nature's second sun.

ELIZABETH HARRISON

Elizabeth [Taylor] says fame is the best deodorant. I say hunger is the best sauce.

RICHARD BURTON

Conservatism is the political equivalent of bed-wetting.

HYWEL WILLIAMS

Someone has described a technicality as a point of principle which we have forgotten.

SIR ELWYN JONES

An actuary is someone who can't stand the excitement of chartered accountancy.

GLAN THOMAS

Critics are misbegotten abortions.

RALPH VAUGHAN WILLIAMS

The finest eloquence is that which gets things done.

DAVID LLOYD GEORGE

A college professor is someone who talks in other people's sleep.

BERGEN EVANS

The happy warrior of Squandermania.
WINSTON CHURCHILL *on David Lloyd George*

Communism is just Puritanism without God.
SAUNDERS LEWIS

The Welsh are the Irish who couldn't swim.
TRADITIONAL SAYING

Feminism is a way of looking at life, not rushing round the kitchen reading bits out of 'Spare Rib'.
DAWN FRENCH

The Hamlet of the sawdust bar.
GWYN THOMAS *on Alf Garnett*

A shouter in lovely dresses.
MARY BENSON *on Shirley Bassey*

Ambition is the grand enemy of all peace.
JOHN COWPER POWYS

A neighbour is someone who has just run out of something.
ROBERT BENCHLEY

'Obscenity' means 'anything that shocks the magistrate'.
BERTRAND RUSSELL

A beautiful doughnut covered in diamonds and paint.
ALAN WILLIAMS' *description of Liz Taylor*

A bank is a place that will lend you money if you can prove that you don't need it.
BOB HOPE

Mass culture is a contradiction in terms.

HUW ELLIS

Trades unions are islands of anarchy in a sea of chaos.

ANEURIN BEVAN

Correct English is the slang of prigs.

GEORGE ELIOT

The Picasso of rugby.

BARRY JOHN *on Carwyn James*

DELUSIONS

The first time Elvis heard Tom Jones sing he couldn't place the Welsh accent. He thought he was black.

MARTY LACKER

Richard Burton was once regaling an interviewer with the story of how his father lost a leg in a mining accident underground but carried on cutting coal until retirement. Fellow countryman and actor, Stanley Baker, also a guest of the interviewer, listened with mounting disbelief, until he finally burst out, 'That wasn't your father, you bastard, it was mine.' Burton turned to him and said calmly, 'What does it matter whose father it was?' And the interview continued as though nothing had happened.

CHRISTOPHER DOWNING

She's as Indian as Paddy's pig.

MARLON BRANDO *on his wife Anna Kashfi. She had pretended she was Indian before they married but he was later to learn that she was really Joan O'Callaghan, the daughter of a Welsh factory worker*

One of their policies was to call everything a tourist attraction and then claim credit for having increased trade. A local hotelier told me that if I was too drunk to drive a horse and spent the night in his hotel I was classified as a tourist.

RICHARD BOOTH *on the Wales Tourist Board in 1978*

Men will put up with anything rather than face the derision of the Smirker. And so the Welsh settlers did what all pioneers do when they arrive and find that the brochure lied. They shivered in crofts made with bricks of turf, and wrote home saying how great everything was. It's another California. Salmon jump from the river into your hand. Birds lay their eggs straight into the frying pan. The rivers are lemon-curded with gold.

MALCOLM PRYCE

He created a wilderness in fairyland, with himself for prophet, and called it Wales.

WYN GRIFFITH *on Caradoc Evans*

Man is a credulous animal and must believe something. In the absence of good grounds for belief he will be satisfied with bad ones.

BERTRAND RUSSELL

When two people collaborate on a book, each believes he gets all the worries and only half the royalties.

AGATHA CHRISTIE

People generally have two reasons for doing something, one that sounds good and the real one.

J P MORGAN

For years I hoped that my mother had picked up the wrong baby in the nursing home and that my real parents would turn up in Fulham to collect me. My real parents were well-educated professionals, who read *The Guardian* over breakfast and listened to chamber music on the radio in the evening. They ate in a dining room and had intelligent conversations about music, politics and foreign countries. Not like my pretend parents, who read the *Daily Mirror*, listened to 'Two-Way Family Favourites' on our radio, and could barely manage a conversation with each other about anything other than our next trip to my grim Nana Bull in Southgate.

JANET STREET-PORTER

People keep telling me they thought I was wonderful in *Naked*, the David Thewlis film. And he gets the same about *Notting Hill*.

RHYS IFANS

I thought *Deep Throat* was about a giraffe.

BOB HOPE

I've only ever kissed a man once. He was a transvestite at one of my shows. He even threw his knickers at me. How could you not be fooled by that?

TOM JONES

DENTOPEDOLOGY

Dentopedology is the science of opening your mouth and putting your foot in it. I've been practising it for years.

PRINCE PHILIP

They've got old shoulders on their heads.

J P R WILLIAMS *in a rugby commentary*

Just enough points here for Tony to pull the cat out of the fire
RAY EDMONDS *during a snooker match*

What State is that in?
GEORGE BUSH *to Charlotte Church after hearing that she was from Wales*

We will definitely improve this year. Last year we lost ten games. This year we only play nine.
RAY JENKINS

You've got to get your first tackle in early, even if it's late.
RAY GRAVELL

Where's Wales?
LOS ANGELES POLICE OFFICER *investigating the death of Rachel Roberts after hearing she was from Wales*

Ian Rush – ready ten times out of ten. But that wasn't one of them.
PETER JONES

Young people, by definition, have their futures before them.
NEIL KINNOCK

Sadly, the immortal Jackie Milburn died recently.
CLIFF MORGAN

Ian Rush is as quick as a needle.
RON JONES

I'm not superstitious – touch wood.
DANNIE ABSE

There was once a sign in a Cardiff haberdashery that said, 'Get Felt Here.'

GORDON IRVING

A rubbery suspect is still holding police at bay in Streatham.

Thames ITV newscaster **TINA JENKINS** *in a 1985 broadcast*

Who is Llewellyn?

PRINCE CHARLES *before his investiture in Caernarfon in 1969 after seeing a banner bearing this moniker of the last Welsh Prince of Wales*

Mr Evans, President of Plaid Cymru for 21 years and a member for 35, was openly moved by his victory. He said, 'It is a tremendous shock, but it was not wholly unexpected.'

THOMAS MYLER

Tell me the truth, were you really mad when you were beaten to the moon by Neil Armstrong?

ALI G *to Buzz Aldrin*

The difference between winning and losing is nothing at all.

TERRY GRIFFITHS

Is there chicken in chickpeas?

HELEN ADAMS *from* Big Brother 2

If you don't believe you can win, there's no point in getting out of bed at the end of the day.

NEVILLE SOUTHALL

Mum, have I sung at the Hollywood Bowl?

CHARLOTTE CHURCH

I turned to see all the onlookers looking on.

ANNEKA RICE

Tell me now, my boy, is this you or your brother?

ELDERLY LADY *to one of her identical grandsons, as remembered by John Edwards*

Ray Reardon, one of the great Crucible champions, won it five times when the championship was played away from the Crucible.

TED LOWE *on the snooker world final*

Before a storm in a tea-cup brews, nip it in the bud.

RUSSELL GRANT

Just enough points here for Tony to pull the cat out of the fire.

RAY EDMONDS

Neville Southall was the finest goalkeeper I ever came up against – even though I always seemed to have the knack of scoring against him.

IAN RUSH

I don't have a normal life, but for me there's nothing in it that isn't normal.

RYAN GIGGS

To his majesty, the King of Sweden!

JAMES CALLAGHAN *toasting the king of Norway*

ECCENTRICITY

Augustus John once patted a child on the head as he passed by him in Chelsea. Asked why he had done so, he replied, 'In case it is one of mine.'

MICHAEL HOLROYD

If Herbert Asquith were buying a large mansion he would come up to you and say, 'Have you thought that there is no room for the cat?'

DAVID LLOYD GEORGE

My pub, the Douglas Arms in Bethesda, Gwynedd, still accepts old money. When decimalisation came in in 1971 I decided not to join.

GEOFFREY DAVIES

J Gwenogfran Evans declared he knew so much about Welsh poetry that he could tell by intuition when words had been added or subtracted by incompetent bards. He corrected texts at will. In one poem of just 6,300 words he made 3,400 changes. Even this is not a complete list.

ADRIAN GILBERT

David Lloyd George spent his whole life plastering together the true and the false and there from manufacturing the plausible.

STANLEY BALDWIN

My favourite book is *The Memoirs of Cleopatra: A Novel*, by Margaret George. It's a thousand pages long. It took me two months to read. When I got to the end, I read it again.

CHARLOTTE CHURCH

The Welshman is a conservative who always votes liberal at elections.

D J NICHOLAS

For Welsh people, the unforgivable eccentricity is to be successful.

JOHN RICHARDS

A great uncle of my wife's once felt it necessary to emigrate to India because he had failed to return a long overdue library book.

DANNIE ABSE

It would seem that when the British live for years in a sweaty climate among foreign people, they maintain their sanity by allowing themselves to go slightly dotty.

ROALD DAHL

I once received a marriage proposal from a total stranger in the post. He enclosed a statement of his assets, and letters from his bank manager.

SIAN PHILLIPS

He could even quote some of Shakespeare's sonnets backwards.

ROSEMARY KINGSLAND *on Richard Burton*

I have carried a whoopee cushion with me since 1975. It's a great ice-breaker.

LESLIE NIELSON

I don't like editing but I write slowly. Sometimes one sentence can take me half an hour.

DICK FRANCIS

I love blinking, I do.

HELEN ADAMS

He's great at sorting out issues of world importance. It's just that he forgets the everyday things like the chords of songs, where he is and so on.

BONO *on his U2 colleague, Edge*

I had left my car parked under some trees alongside the St. George Hotel, where I was staying. When I went to drive to the Crucible it was covered in pigeon droppings. After beating Perrie Mans I decided it must have been a lucky omen so for the rest of the tournament I religiously parked under the same trees

TERRY GRIFFITHS *on the year he won the World Snooker Championship*

One of the most horrible eccentricities ever indulged in was that of John Donne, who, in his later years, became so preoccupied with the thought of death that for the last portrait to be painted of him he insisted on standing in a coffin and wrapping himself in a white shroud.

DYLAN THOMAS

In Detroit we met a dealer in film books who had amputated one of his fingers to get compensation from his health insurance. The money enabled him to make a horror film about a bed that ate people.

RICHARD BOOTH

I no longer keep the coal in the bath. I keep it in the bidet.

JOHN PRESCOTT

I say, old son, you're doing very well. but should you be trying to change gear with the handbrake?

HUGH GRIFFITH *to Peter O'Toole, during a holiday in the west of Ireland*

One of his favourite sports was to go out on the road and attack passing cars with his bare fists.

ELIZABETH HARRISON *on Richard Harris*

EISTEDDFODAU

The Eisteddfod is a wonderful occasion where musicians, singers and dancers from all over the world gather together and have great fun trying to pronounce Llangollen correctly.

GREN JONES

The great dynasty of preachers shaped our soul and established the rules of our not inconsiderable rhetoric. And behind the Preacher has always stood the image of the powerfully literate ploughman and miner, who have given to our working people an impressive and articulate dignity. That is why the Eisteddfod cuts so deep into our social earth.

GWYN THOMAS

The eisteddfod is a kind of washing machine into which the Welsh toss their psyches, to be scrubbed and ready for another year's battling.

TREVOR FISHLOCK

Long-term expats latch on to the eisteddfod for their quick fix of Welshness.

BETHAN KILFOIL

Outside Wales the eisteddfod is regarded as a procession of bards from a miniature Stonehenge to a crowded pavilion where thousands of Welsh people burst into hymn-singing on the slightest provocation.

WYN GRIFFITH

I would like to read a Welsh author not mentioning (a) the harmonium, and (b) Eisteddfods.

MARGIAD EVANS

The National Eisteddfod is racial intolerance set to music.

SKIDMORE

THE ENGLISH AND THE WELSH

It is easy to love Wales when you are far away from it, making a fortune in England.

W J GRUFFYDD

The relationship between the Welsh and the English is based on trust and understanding. They don't trust us and we don't understand them.

DUDLEY WOOD

No Englishman can understand the Welsh. However much he may try, however sympathetic he may feel, he cannot get inside the skin and bones of a Welshman, unless he be born again.

LADY MEGAN LLOYD GEORGE

The sad fact must be faced that we are even more boring to the English than they are to us, which is saying a great deal.

HARRI WEBB

Eddy was a tremendously tolerant person, but he wouldn't put up with the Welsh. He always said, 'Surely there's enough English to go round.'

JOHN MORTIMER

We can trace all the disasters of English history to the influence of the Welsh.

EVELYN WAUGH

There seemed at one time to be complete justification for the notorious entry in one of the early editions of the *Encyclopaedia Britannica* – 'For Wales see England'. Yet Wales steadfastly refused to disappear politely from the map.

WYNFORD VAUGHAN-THOMAS

> When it comes to the great scorer
> To mark against your name
> He'll not ask you how you played the game
> but – whether you beat England.

MAX BOYCE

Once, when sitting with my father in the trap on his way down to Mostyn for a beer, I asked what that place was over the water, with all that sand. He said it was another country where Welsh was not spoken and the public houses were open on Sunday.

EMLYN WILLIAMS

Look what those English bastards have done to Wales. They've taken our coal, our water, our steel. They buy our houses and only live in them for a fortnight every year. And what have they given us in return? Absolutely nothing. We've been exploited, raped, controlled and punished by them – and that's who you're playing this afternoon.

Speech given by **PHIL BENNETT** *prior to a Wales-England rugby clash in 1977*

Go into any bookshop in Wales and you will be in England.

RHYS DAVIES

Englishmen were born to rule and not to be ruled – least of all by a bumptious, snuffling, flighty, tiresome, fifth-rate bunch of barbarians like the Welsh.

T W CROSLAND

There is a Welshman hidden in many an Englishman.

ENOCH POWELL

The very geological structure of Wales has moulded its agriculture and its industry. Over everything looms the all-powerful presence of an ambitious England.

WYNFORD VAUGHAN-THOMAS

When I'm in England I tell people I'm Welsh, and when I'm in Wales I tell people I'm English.

DYLAN THOMAS

The Welsh people have been oppressed for 500 years by the English State – but then so have the English people.

RAYMOND WILLIAMS

England includes Wales but not Scotland.

SIR DONALD SOMERVILLE

If there were 600 angels in Westminster they would be English angels and they would be unable to understand how Wales thinks.

CLEDWYN HUGHES

The reason Monty Python works so well is because John Cleese has that Anglo-Saxon repression and I'm a mad Welshman. I threw a chair at him once.

TERRY JONES

'Do you,' an exasperated Englishman is said to have asked a Welsh shopkeeper, 'have a word in your language that is equivalent to the Spanish term *mañana*?' 'Nothing,' the Welshman replied, 'that conveys quite the same sense of urgency.'

TREVOR FISHLOCK

Keep Wales Tidy. Dump your rubbish in England.

CAR STICKER

The Anglo-Welsh, though they are a danger to the Welsh language, must never be its enemy, and the Welsh Welsh, even if they are the true dancers before our tribal ark, will be unwise to try to impose an irresistible logic upon an immovable fact.

GWYN JONES

>Two lands at last connected
>Across the rivers wide,
>And all the tools collected
>On the English side.

HARRI WEBB's ode to the *Severn Bridge*

Wales, Scotland and Ireland all have a similar relationship with England – she's been two-timing all of us.

YNYR JONES

Of course the people of Wales have an inferiority complex. What would you expect? We've spent 500 years looking up England's backside and seeing the sun shine out of it.

DOLGELLAU DWELLER *to Trevor Fishlock*

The famous clock in Chester has only three faces. The one facing Wales is missing for a reason. As we all know, the people of Chester wouldn't give the Welsh the time of day.

EMYR LLOYD

In England, to be Welsh is a decided shortcoming. A Welsh pearl is a fake, a Welsh cricket is a louse, Welsh parsley is a noose, a Welshman's hug is an itch.

PAMELA PETRO

The history of Welsh writing is brief. It is enough to remind the reader that no Thackeray, Dickens, Trollope, Arnold Bennett or H G Wells has written a novel about Wales.

WYN GRIFFITH

The law of libel, of English origin and an affair of expensive lawyers and a frightening court judge, is rarely invoked in Wales. It is the local social law that is used, and the punishment for being judged guilty of offending against it can be none the less effective; no heavy fines, but ostracism, disgrace and the hostile gaze that can isolate a person into an eternal prison and gradually turn his substance into rot.

RHYS DAVIES

English has been pushing into Wales for the last generation. It used to be said that the line of cleavage, at one point, ran down the middle of a village street.

A G BRADLEY

EXHIBITIONISTS

Back in Wales our family would always provide their own entertainment. Everyone stood up and did a turn, going back generations. Something of that went straight through to David.

OLWEN JASON *on her famous son David*

It is a truth universally acknowledged that a Welshman in possession of an audience of at least one, a pint of best and a complete set of vocal chords, can never be in want of something to say.

CHRISTOPHER DOWNING

The Welsh are all actors; it's only the bad ones who become professionals.

RICHARD BURTON

Why do I gyrate on stage? Because people want it. It's like a boxer who finds his left hook is working better than anything else.

TOM JONES

I was at Elton John's for his birthday party. It was slightly bigger than the estate I grew up on.

CRAIG DAVID

Fame is only a barometer of the television programme most widely watched.

RICHARD MADELEY

T E Lawrence had a genius for backing into the limelight.

LOWELL THOMAS

I haven't spoken to my mother-in-law for eighteen months. I don't like to interrupt her.

KEN DODD

The place was so English I wouldn't be surprised if the mice wore monocles.

BOB HOPE

FAME

You may be a big shot up in London, but down here in Pontypridd you wipe your shoes when you come in and take your turn bringing in the coal.

The first words of **TOM JONES' MOTHER** *to him after he became famous*

Catherine Zeta-Jones, suing *Hello* magazine, took Iraq off the front pages. That says a lot about our obsession with nonentities.

MATTHEW PARIS

Nothing can be done for a genius. Unfortunately, nature does not mark him at birth or we could soon put an end to him and not only save the State work, but, better still, save him from the cruel sport of fame.

W H DAVIES

I once caught two fans looking into my bedroom window. It was scary.

GAVIN HENSON

Television turned all our cues into magic wands.

Snooker ace **RAY REARDON**

These days a star is anyone who can hold a microphone. A superstar is someone who has shaken hands with Lew Grade, and a super-superstar is the man who has refused to shake hands with Lew Grade.

HARRY SECOMBE *in 1972*

To have news value is to have a tin can tied to one's tail.

T E LAWRENCE

My family keeps me grounded by making me do housework.

CHARLOTTE CHURCH

Celebrity opens doors and lowers drawers.

EDDIE IZZARD

I sometimes pinch myself. It's a long way from washing pots and pans for a living to be able to pop round to Madonna's house at the bottom of the road, press the button and hear her call, 'Hi. Vinnie, come in. I'll put the kettle on.'

VINNIE JONES

I could sign 999 autographs and, after that, if I didn't sign one more it could be held against me.

RYAN GIGGS

It is a mark of our time that more and more people step into the spotlight of world fame at an absurdly early age. Some of them make it so young that, at thirty, they are already senile anachronisms.

GWYN THOMAS

FOOD

In Wales we subsisted mostly on trout which we poached from a stream. We would take an enormous grand piano down and place it on the bank, and then someone would play *The Moonlight Sonata* which, of course, makes trout rise to the surface. Then we would bash the buggers on the head with a banana. One Welshman became so stout on trout and bananas that, when he died, they couldn't get him out of his cottage to bury him.

RICHARD BURTON *in one of his drunken fantasies*

I have secretly worried about being hooked on welsh-cakes. I will, in all probability, join 'Welsh-cakes Anonymous' some day and be urged to talk to others about my problem. No doubt there will be the inevitable death from such an addiction, and the story carried in the local paper back home: 'Max Boyce, formerly of 37 Cemetery Road, Tonypandy, was found dead in his apartment in the early hours of yesterday morning. He left a son and two welsh-cakes.'

MAX BOYCE

In Aberffraw earlier this year the fish and chip shop closed. Which, in Wales, means the end of the world cannot be far off.

BYRON ROGERS

Breakfast cereal is made up of all those little curly wooden shavings you find in pencil sharpeners.

ROALD DAHL

He could coax a meal from a brick wall if the mortar were soft enough.

GWYN THOMAS *on W.H. Davies*

There are only two types of women in the world: those who love chocolate and complete bitches.

DAWN FRENCH

I went into a French restaurant and asked the waiter if he had frogs' legs. When he said he had, I said, 'Well hop into the kitchen and get me a cheese sandwich.'

TOMMY COOPER

The greatest drawback in making pictures is the fact that film-makers have to eat.

RAY MILLAND

I used to go to a restaurant where you could eat as much as you wanted for a given fee. They closed down.

HARRY SECOMBE

The only food outlets in Wales which aren't run by Italians are those which sell pizzas.

JOHN RICHARDS

I'd love to witness that virgin moment when a baby first has chocolate.

DAWN FRENCH

Elvis used to go on eating binges but he would kid himself it was all right because he was exercising. He wasn't, of course. He'd got one of those exercise bikes but the pedals were driven by an electric motor. He'd be sitting on the bike, which was pedalling itself, eating wedges of pizza. 'Yeah, Tom,' he'd say, deadly serious, 'I like to keep in shape.'

TOM JONES

I eat at this German–Chinese restaurant and the food is delicious; the only problem is that an hour later you're hungry for power.

DICK CAVETT

I can't even *spell* diet.

GARETH EDWARDS

Ireland was grand. I ate myself daft.

DYLAN THOMAS

This year we took our holiday in the south of France. My schoolboy French has deteriorated. I had to leave all conversations to my wife. One must shut up irrevocably if, on asking for bread at a restaurant, one is served with rabbit.

DANNIE ABSE

A man may be talking the most sublime sense imaginable but one listens to it less attentively if he suspends the flow from time to time to spread a good inch of cream cheese on to a cracker.

GWYN THOMAS

It was with Columbo that I opened King's restaurant. The idea came to us when we were trying to decide where to go to eat one day. One of us wanted one thing and the other wanted something else. In the end one of us said the only way round it was to open our own restaurant. We both claimed to have had the idea first when it was a success but gave credit to the other when it collapsed.

JOHN CHARLES

FOOTBALL

I'd rather go home and play for Flint Town United.

IAN RUSH *after failing to settle in Italy with Juventus in 1988*

I once scored a goal at football, but it was for the other side.

HARRY SECOMBE

I'm sweating more blood on the bench than some of the players on the field.

JOHN TOSHACK IN 1989

If you have a fortnight's holiday in Dublin you qualify to play for the national side.

MIKE ENGLAND

When we played football at school I was usually put in goal – basically because I filled most of it.

JANET BRYANT

I gave a little squeeze. Genteelly, of course. Gazza didn't squeal. Well, not a lot. I think he tried to but no sound came out.

VINNIE JONES *on the infamous time he was photographed holding onto Paul Gascoigne's 'wotsits' during a match*

I wouldn't go as far as to say Neville Southall is a complete nutcase, but he comes pretty close.

TERRY YORATH

If he fouls you he normally picks you up, but the referee doesn't see what he picks you up by.

RYAN GIGGS *on Dennis Wise*

Certain people are for me, certain people are pro me.

TERRY VENABLES

Ask any striker what was the greatest goal he ever scored and they'll all give you the same answer – the next one.

IAN RUSH

Gentlemen, these people bombed your houses, killed your mothers and fathers and brothers and sisters. Go out and get your own back.

Pre-match injunction by **JIMMY MURPHY** *to his team when they played against Germany in the aftermath of World War II*

HEALTH

God and the doctor we alike adore
But only when in danger, not before;
The danger o'er, both are alike requited,
God is forgotten, and the doctor slighted.

JOHN OWEN

All the Welsh are systematically lumbered with are copious Giros and repeat prescriptions of pessaries for ovine cystitis.

A A GILL

I had measles so quickly on top of chicken pox, the spots were fighting each other for space.

HARRY SECOMBE

I always get an attack of piles on the third week of shooting, and my back slips.

RICHARD BURTON

'One finger in the throat and one in the rectum makes a good diagnostician,' the consultant said, quoting Sir William Osier, and some of us remembered another saying of Osier's which was, 'Look wise say nothing, and grunt.' I often had to grunt when cross-examined on ward rounds.

DANNIE ABSE *on his time as a junior doctor*

I only get ill when I give up drugs.

KEITH RICHARDS

I went to see the doctor the other day. I had to. He wasn't well.

TOMMY COOPER

Insanity runs in my family. In fact, it gallops.

CARY GRANT

He's worn out two bodies already,

RAY REARDON *on Alex Higgins*

My brother Terry's in an asylum right now. I'd like to believe the insanity is because our family is all genius, but I'm afraid that's not true. Some of them – a good many – are just nice nobodies. I'm quite fond of insanity, actually. It's a nice thing to throw out at parties. Everybody finds empathy in a nutty family. Everybody says, 'Oh, yes, my family is quite mad'. But mine really is.

DAVID BOWIE IN 1976

I think I've coped well with Alzheimer's Disease, which, of course, becomes progressively worse. It has been a bit of a pest but I don't worry about it. If I sing the same song again at the bar, what does it matter? People just have to put up with it.

JOHN CHARLES

HIRAETH

Hiraeth is a kind of longing that is more than simple homesickness because you can get it at home too. It's a lament not only for what has been lost, but for what should have been but never was: a weary and, so far, an impotent protest that history hasn't played fair.

PAMELA PETRO

It has always amused me that so many Welsh people, when they move away from the Principality, suddenly become very conscious of their Welshness. At the end of every concert during my overseas tours there will be a very nice Welsh lady waiting for me. She will be carrying a biscuit tin covered loosely with a blue check tablecloth, and behind her, at a Sunday school distance, will be her husband, wearing a sheepish grin, red socks, and a faded Triple Crown tie.

MAX BOYCE

When I was eighteen, if you dialled Pontypridd 3667, the local telephone box, the chances were you'd have got me in that box. It was my first home, my first office. I courted girls from it. My family began in it – not literally, mind you. It was as much part of my life as my first gold record.

TOM JONES *who subsequently had the box flown to his home in the US for nostalgic reasons*

Rural Wales is where I belong, but I don't want to live in it. I want to have it to go back to.

EMLYN WILLIAMS

You never get over *hiraeth*. It's like tearing bits of your skin off every time you leave.

RICHARD BURTON

I left Pontypridd but it never left me.

ALUN RICHARDS

Richard was married on the day of a rugby international. Wales was playing Scotland. The bridegroom and his buddies decided to watch it on television. Worse than that, Wales lost. You never saw such a disgruntled wedding party in your life.

PHILIP BURTON *on his namesake*

After I won the World Championship, I went back to my old club and put my name on the board, the way I always used to do. It wasn't accepted. They thought I was being falsely humble. I couldn't go back again. I was the world champion and nothing would ever be the same for me.

TERRY GRIFFITHS *after becoming snooker champion of the world in 1979*

Among restless souls down the centuries there goes an insistent refrain like a drumbeat: 'When I am at home, I wish I were abroad, and when I am abroad, I wish I were at home.'

EMYR HUMPHREYS

When I am shaving in the morning, I say to myself that if I were a young man I would emigrate, but by the time I am sitting down to breakfast, I ask myself, 'Where would I go?'

JAMES CALLAGHAN

If I had been pulled off the streets of Belfast at fifteen years old and hurled onto the pitch at Old Trafford, I feel I'd have ended up like George Best. I was able to stay in my natural environment and develop there as a respected member of the community.

BARRY JOHN

HOLLYWOOD

Hollywood likes old Englishmen. It doesn't have much use for old English women. No disrespect, but there was old Cedric Hardwicke. He had a naughty nickname, Sir Seldom Hardprick. He had a thriving career in Tinsel Town, despite having the personality and drive of an old tortoise hunting for lettuce.

RACHEL ROBERTS

Many people believe Hollywood is 'it', the epitome. They don't question. I love what Gandhi said when he arrived in England from India and a pompous journalist asked him, 'What do you think about western civilisation?' He replied, 'I think it would be an excellent idea'.

RICHARD BURTON

The Hollywood of the Fifties dampened my spirits. It was wonderful to discover that there was another world, inhabited by foreign movie actors who looked just like people, only more so.

SIAN PHILLIPS

If my agent calls for me to do anything, it's always mad fat girls, mothers of eight, or matrons.

DAWN FRENCH

There was always a greater standard of acting at Hollywood parties than in Hollywood films.

BETTE DAVIS

I was reluctant to work in Hollywood. I was afraid the neighbours might think I was showing off.

EMLYN WILLIAMS

I hadn't a clue what I was talking about most of the time.

DESMOND LLEWELLYN, *who played the Secret Service gadget 'expert' in the James Bond movies*

Wise Hollywood hostesses never invited columnists to their parties because once you did you could never leave them off your list for future parties or they would crucify you.

RAY MILLAND

You've got to swank it in Hollywood. When I go there I demand two Cadillacs and the best dressing-room. Of course, I'm not worth it, but it impresses them.

RICHARD BURTON

The trouble with Hollywood is that it ain't got culture.

VINCENT PRICE

Hollywood had a readymade, unchanging market to satisfy in the 1930s and the product had to be available. To a tardy director of a potboiler pleading for more time to complete a better picture, the producer shouted: 'I don't want it good. I want it Thursday.'

HUGH LOUDON

Even when in old age he faced that vast Hollywood throng, baring its heart in shamed apology for America's virtual banishment of a staggeringly creative man, he still looked as if he was standing insecurely on the surface of an alien planet.

GWYN THOMAS *on Charlie Chaplin*

Cameron Diaz looks pretty good despite the fact that she doesn't come from Wales.

GLYN DAVIES

IDEAS

Rebels grow to love the things which first prompted their rebellion,

GWYN THOMAS

Doctrinaires are the vultures of principle. They feed upon it after it is dead.

DAVID LLOYD GEORGE

An expert is a man who has stopped thinking. Why should he think? He is an expert.

FRANK LLOYD WRIGHT

There was never a good war or a bad peace.

BENJAMIN FRANKLIN

Every murderer is probably somebody's old friend.

AGATHA CHRISTIE

A toothache can sometimes be cured by laying out a few old copies of *Punch* on your dining-table.

HUW WHELDON

It's a pity we can't suffer our illnesses when we're young and healthy.

MAX ABSE

Innocence is always a paradox.

VERNON WATKINS

I wonder what it was like to be Shakespeare.

DICK FRANCIS

Moral sentiment corrupts the young. Children are the first to lose their innocence; artists the second; idiots never.

AUGUSTUS JOHN

There is nothing will kill a man as soon as having nobody to find fault with but himself.

GEORGE ELIOT

Often it's more important to win one person over than a hundred.

GWYNFOR EVANS

Experience can only be gathered by living. I've never yet met a good actor who got it all from early nights and Stanislavski.

ELIZABETH HARRISON

The real world is not always easy to live in but there's nothing quite so unendurable as persistent unreality.

ELIZABETH HARRISON

IDENTITY

The idea of some people being more Welsh than others comes from the fact that the bellwether of the country's fate, the Welsh language, was fractured long ago, on the hard rocks of English, into an emotionally charged hierarchy of subsets.

PAMELA PETRO

When I went to England I was aware of being Welsh. In Italy I was aware of being British. In America I was aware of being European. And in the House of Commons I was aware of being female.

BETHAN KILFOIL

Anyone can choose to be Welsh as long as they're prepared to take the consequences.

GLYN JONES

Until the First World War, the ordinary Welshman was not aware of any difficulty in being Welsh.

WYN GRIFFITH

The first thing to realise about the Welsh is that they're not really Welsh at all. They're the real Britons.

HV MORTON

Of course I was entitled to be in *Under Milk Wood*. Why not? I have a Welsh wife, a Welsh mother-in-law and two half-Welsh children. I had to learn Welsh, to speak with my family. That is more than Dylan Thomas can say. He couldn't speak a single word of Welsh.

PETER O'TOOLE *on the 1973 film of Thomas' most famous work.*

IMAGE

A spoiled genius from the Welsh gutter, a drinker, a womaniser. It's rather an attractive image.

RICHARD BURTON

People simply do not seem to understand that I'm an actor and in real life most gadgets expire or explode as soon as I touch them. I can barely change a light bulb, let alone repair the toaster.

DESMOND LLEWELLYN

She was a blonde with a brunette past.

GWYN THOMAS

Rex Harrison was nicer to his leading ladies than his wives. They got the pleasant public face while the wives got the cold reality. If we hadn't been shackled together he'd have flirted with me on the set just for his credentials.

RACHEL ROBERTS

The idea that there is a model Labour voter, a blue-collar council house tenant who belongs to a union and has 2.4 children, a five-year-old car and a holiday in Blackpool, is patronising and politically immature.

NEIL KINNOCK

People never talk about my music. They just count how many pairs of knickers are thrown at me during my performance.

TOM JONES

The media play tricks with the truth. They've had me pregnant a few times, engaged a few more, and generally falling out of nightclubs blotto. The truth is my nana has a more exciting social life than I have.

CHARLOTTE CHURCH

He went to America to play Dylan Thomas.

CONSTANCE FITZGIBBON *on Thomas*

I think I even pose when sleeping.

KYLIE MINOGUE

I could never understand why Joe Louis was World Champion when everyone knew Humphrey Bogart was the toughest guy in the world.

ANTHONY HOPKINS

We try to avoid being a celebrity couple as much as possible. I can't think of anything more sick-making. Most nights I sit in with a chicken wing, watching *EastEnders*.

DAWN FRENCH *on herself and her husband, Lenny Henry*

Many a dumb blonde is really a smart brunette.

GWILYM DAVIES

Film stars never stubbed their toes on loose paving stones. They never fluffed their lines. Their houses had bathrooms but you never ever saw a lavatory pan. They really were like extra-terrestrial beings. Did they go to the toilet like the rest of us?

HUGH LOUDON *on his childhood impressions of Hollywood*

I heard one man say to another a little while ago, 'Who did you say he was? Dick Francis? Oh, yes, he's the man who didn't win the National.' What an epitaph!

DICK FRANCIS

In his youth, William Wordsworth sympathised with the French Revolution, wrote good poetry and had a natural daughter. At this period he was a 'bad' man. Then, he became 'good', abandoned his daughter, adopted correct principles, and wrote bad poetry.

BERTRAND RUSSELL

Perhaps if I dyed my hair peroxide blonde and called myself 'The Great White Tadpole', people would take more notice of me.

IAN WOOSNAM

I've got so many shells I've forgotten what the pea looks like.

DAVID BOWIE

INSULTS

Someone once spray-painted the legend 'Harry Secombe is a wanker' on the wall outside my house. Between finding the graffiti and arranging to have it removed, my knighthood was announced. The next day, the artist added to his handiwork, which now read, 'Sir Harry Secombe is a wanker.'

HARRY SECOMBE

How many Bridgend fans can you fit into a Ford Fiesta? Answer: All of them!

JONATHAN JENKINS

If you took off your spectacles and sat on the fire, the room would be full of the smell of roast pork.

DYLAN THOMAS *to a bore at a party*

'Wales?' a taxi driver in New York said, screwing up his face. 'D'ya mean da fish or dem singin' bastards?

TREVOR FISHLOCK

You were a weak, pale, pusillanimous imitation of Laurence Olivier.

MEREDITH JONES *to Richard Burton after listening to him doing 'Henry V' on BBC Radio*

Anne Robinson suffers from that calamitous condition that compels her to get up and trash a fellow female a day in order to feel fulfilled.

JANET STREET-PORTER *after Robinson cast aspersions on Cherie Blair's dress sense*

All the world is queer save thee and me, and even thou art a little queer.

ROBERT OWEN *to William Allen upon terminating business relations with him in 1828*

Dramatic art, in Jayne Mansfield's opinion, is knowing how to fill a sweater.

BETTE DAVIS

She's the sort of woman who lives for others, and you can tell the others by their hunted expression.

C S LEWIS

A wig-wearing, numerical incompetent, incapable of matching a tie and jacket, let alone remembering contestants' names.

CAROL VORDERMAN's *fond jibe to Richard Whiteley, her 'Countdown' colleague*

I don't know how old the plane was, but Lindbergh's lunch was still on the seat. The path to the washroom was outside.

BOB HOPE

Might that not have been a case of helping a lame dog over a stile?

MAX BEERBOHM *to W H Davies, after hearing he had received a leg-up on the poetry ladder from George Bernard Shaw*

Abu Dhabi has always sounded to me like a disease.

MAX BOYCE

Augustus John is the best bad painter in Britain.

PABLO PICASSO

The part calls for an actor who can convey somebody savage and uncouth. You should play it.

JOHN GIELGUD *to Emlyn Williams while casting 'The Laughing Woman'*

There has never been a divorce in the Dahl family, but infidelity is accepted.

PATRICIA NEAL, *on the double standards of her author husband Roald Dahl*

Muhammad Ali wouldn't have hit Joe Louis on the bum with a handful of rice.

TOMMY FARR

'He's so fucking square,' he complained, 'he must have come out of a cubic womb.' It was a gynaecological opinion I shared.

ELIZABETH HARRISON *agreeing with Richard Harris about Charlton Heston*

INTELLIGENCE

The typical Welsh intellectual is only one generation away from shirt-sleeves.

RAYMOND WILLIAMS

The cleverness of Welsh graduates has nothing to bite on except the national grievance.

MEIC STEPHENS

A great intellect may be able to produce great prose, but not a line of poetry.

EDWARD THOMAS

He's incredibly loyal. Ask him to jump off the stand roof and he'll do it. But he's as thick as two short planks. He always grabbed the quiz book on our coach trips so he could ask the questions. That way he didn't have to answer them.

Physiotherapist **ARNIE REED** *on Vinnie Jones*

It was eighty degrees in the shade today but I was clever. I stayed in the sun.

TOMMY COOPER

Intelligence does little to help you get through life.

RACHEL GRIFFITHS

The average man's opinions are much less foolish than they would be if he thought for himself.

BERTRAND RUSSELL

Catherine Zeta-Jones has her brain screwed the right way. She married a rich pensioner.

MAKOSI *from* Big Brother 6

You cannot fashion a wit out of two half-wits.

NEIL KINNOCK

IRONY

The Welsh are so damn Welsh that it looks like an affectation.

SIR ALEXANDER RALEIGH

I found myself in jail in Italy on what would have been the day of my second wedding.

JOHN CHARLES, *after a tax problem reared its ugly head*

In the old days everyone was so one-eyed they would applaud me in the red of Wales one week, cheering every successful kick, and boo me the following Saturday, if I was playing for Cardiff at Newport, Llanelli or Swansea willing me to miss every kick.

BARRY JOHN

It's sometimes said that to try to keep Wales bilingual is merely to postpone the day on which Welsh disappears.

WYN GRIFFITH

My temperature had reached 101 degrees Fahrenheit. I felt as hot as Port Talbot Steelworks. Nauseous, too. For a moment, as I reclined in bed, I wondered whether I should consult a doctor. 'I *am* a doctor,' I reminded myself.

DANNIE ABSE

The insurance man told me the accident policy covered me falling off the roof but not hitting the ground.

TOMMY COOPER

If I did not enjoy riding horses that do not win, I could not be a jockey.

DICK FRANCIS

If you give up trying to possess what attracts you, a lovely, thrilling happiness flows through you and you feel you're in touch with the secret of everything.

JOHN COWPER POWYS

A marriage is likely to be called happy if neither party ever expected to get much happiness out of it.

BERTRAND RUSSELL

LANGUAGE

The language is even more important for Wales than self-government.

SAUNDERS LEWIS

Losing my Welsh temper meant gaining my Welsh accent.

EMLYN WILLIAMS

The Welsh language is complicated but euphonious. People think it has no vowels but the contrary is true. It is almost all vowels, and they run off the tongue like oil by diphthongs and triphtongs.

GERARD MANLEY HOPKINS

If a Welshman has anything of real importance to say he must say it in English.

MATTHEW ARNOLD

The Welsh are brilliant. Who else could have revived a long-dead and very silly language which was only useful for telling complex and profitable lies?

MICHAEL BYWATER

If Welsh goes, a bastardised vernacular will take its place.

KATE ROBERTS

Aneurin Bevan was the only man I ever knew who could make a curse sound like a caress.

MICHAEL FOOT

Even the non Welsh-speaking Welshmen owe their Welshness to the Welsh language.

DAFYDD IWAN

We retired to a hostelry. There, two old men were engaged in a fierce argument in Welsh. The barmaid whispered to this monoglot, 'They're on about the meaning of life.' I listened further and identified some names, which revealed to me that they were talking about rugby.

DANNIE ABSE

I regret not having learned Welsh. Even my father's gradually became rusty, living with a monoglot mother.

GEOFFREY HOWE

I gave up drinking after I realised Welsh had become my second language after slurring.

BRYN EDWARDS

Is our obsession with the Welsh language an acknowledgement of the fact that we are too late to save it?

R S THOMAS

Darned garrulous lot, these Welsh. Just haven't given the lingo a chance to lie decently down and die.

TOURIST *overheard by Gwyn Thomas in a hotel*

The first Welsh phrase I heard was when someone said, 'I'll take your coat in case it rains, isn't it?' Isn't it what?' I asked. The second phrase I heard was, 'There's cold your hands are.'

MICHAEL ASPEL

Welshness and the Welsh language aren't synonymous. A Welshman is a Welshman before he becomes a Welsh speaker.

GWYN JONES

Now I perceive the devil understands Welsh.

WILLIAM SHAKESPEARE

There is no verb meaning 'to have' in Welsh. Plane tickets, maps, languages even, are only 'with you'. This pattern of having things 'with you' seems to me a grammar built on loss and impermanence, the linguistic heritage of the defeated.

PAMELA PETRO

My father's mother knew only one word of English: Damn.

GEORGE THOMAS

The Welsh alphabet is locked in a perpetual game of musical chairs from hell.

PAMELA PETRO

DAVID LLOYD GEORGE INSULTS

Neville Chamberlain has a retail mind in a wholesale business. He might make an adequate Lord Mayor of Birmingham in a lean year.

Ramsay Macdonald has sufficient conscience to bother him, but not sufficient to keep him straight.

Neville Chamberlain saw foreign policy through the wrong end of a municipal drainpipe.

William Haig is brilliant – to the top of his boots.

The Right Honourable gentleman has sat so long on the fence, the iron has entered his soul.

Lord Kitchener is like one of those revolving lighthouses which radiate momentary gleams of light far out into the surrounding gloom and then suddenly relapse into complete darkness.

When they circumcised Herbert Samuel, they threw away the wrong bit.

Arthur Balfour's impact on history is no more than the whiff of scent on a lady's handkerchief.

An alliance with Lord Northcliffe is like going for a walk with a grasshopper.

Lord Gladstone is a pygmy posturing before the footlights in the road of a giant.

MARRIAGE

Dai: I hear Myfanwy is getting married.
Gwyn: I didn't know she was pregnant.
Dai: She's not.
Gwyn: Ooh – there's posh!
DAI OWEN

After the longest engagement In Welsh history, Dai eventually said to Gwladys, 'Don't you think it's time we got married?' To which she replied, 'Who would have us, at our age?'
WYNFORD JONES

Welshmen haven't kissed their wives for years, but will thump anyone else who tries to do it.
EMYR LLOYD

I find it impossible to conceive of spending a whole day with someone, let along getting married to them.

CHRISTIAN BALE

Movie stars and monogamy go together like cornflakes and Tabasco.

JULIA LLEWELLYN SMITH

I don't break up marriages, I strengthen them. When women see me on stage they go back home to their husbands charged up like teenagers again.

TOM JONES

The married life of Shirley Bassey and Kenneth Hume was unusual. To begin with, they did not live together.

MURIEL BURGESS

I was married three days ago to Caitlin Macnamara in Penzance registry office with no money, no prospect of money, no attendant friends or relatives, and in complete happiness.

DYLAN THOMAS *in a telegram to Vernon Watkins in 1937*

If I had to make the choice between staying married and playing snooker, snooker would win.

RAY REARDON

Even in civilised mankind, faint traces of the monogamous instinct can be perceived.

BERTRAND RUSSELL

Marriage is neither heaven nor hell. It is simply purgatory.

ABRAHAM LINCOLN

Marriage may often be a stormy lake but celibacy is almost always a muddy horse-pond.

THOMAS LOVE PEACOCK

'He married her to get rid of her' was an Irish saying I knew and recognised,

SIAN PHILLIPS

Has that fat little Jewish tart turned up yet? I swear she'll be late for the last bloody judgment.

RICHARD BURTON *on his wedding day when Liz Taylor failed to show on time*

Marriage is like throwing yourself in the river when you only want a drink.

DAVID JASON

What with mortgages becoming steeper than the Himalayas and pork chops as rare and dear as uranium, it is possible to speculate that wedlock will shortly be replaced by a loosely organised promiscuity, and the traditional family homestead by a corner in a youth hostel, with the youths touching ninety and wearing shorts, not because they wish to suggest an abiding enthusiasm for fitness, but because they cannot afford the rest of the trousers.

GWYN THOMAS

I didn't just marry Peter O'Toole. I married his country as well.

SIAN PHILLIPS

I've been happily married for ten years. Unfortunately, I've been married for twenty.

HILDA INGLIS

Bachelors believe in the happiness of pursuit.

WYN JENKINS

As I got ready for bed, Roald turned to me and nonchalantly said, 'Pat, I want a divorce. This marriage is the wrong thing for both of us.' I was absolutely dumbfounded. We had been married less than eight months. 'But don't worry about it now,' he said, 'just go to sleep'.

PATRICIA NEAL *on Roald Dahl*

It was a really nice occasion and I wish our children had been there to see it.

DANNIE ABSE *on his wedding*

MEN AND WOMEN

There are so many guys out here with huge egos. Still, I prefer Hollywood dating to the Welsh version. Where I come from it's, 'Do you want a pint of Guinness and a packet of crisps? I've got a transit van in the car park.' At least here, I'm taken out for dates on a private jet.

CATHERINE ZETA-JONES *before she met Michael Douglas*

A real Welshman will admire Miss World for her politics.

GREN JONES

I love her not for her breasts or her buttocks but her mind. It is inscrutable. She is like a poem.

RICHARD BURTON *on Liz Taylor*

What inconsiderate buggers we males are.

AUGUSTUS JOHN

American boys in films always gave flowers to their girlfriends when they collected them for a date. This convulsed us in uncontrollable laughter. In Pontypridd, we might offer her a sweet if she was lucky.

HUGH LOUDON

Hundreds of men love more than one woman.

DYLAN THOMAS

Diamonds never leave you. Men do.

SHIRLEY BASSEY

This *caru-ar-y-gwely*, called courting on the bed, is customary throughout Wales. The girl sits on the bed chatting with her boyfriend until morning.

JULIUS RODENBERG

There's no more irresistible mating call than the imperious horn at the kerb.

BERGEN EVANS

Men are vey funny. If I had one of those dangly things stuffed down the front of my pants I'd stay at home all day laughing at myself.

DAWN FRENCH

Woman is made for man. Man is made for life.

RICHARD BURTON

What is the proper function of women if it is not to make reasons for husbands to stay at home, and still stronger ones for bachelors to go out?

GEORGE ELIOT

I would love to go to board meetings where he is chairman but I'm not invited. I guess it wouldn't be right for me to differ with him. But at home it's the petticoat rule.

LAURA ASHLEY *on her relationship to her husband Bernard*

I still chase women – but only when they're running downhill.

BOB HOPE

MISPRINTS

Then one of the newer Labour MPs rushed across the floor to shake a clenched fish in the Prime Minister's face.

WESTERN MAIL

Armed with a combination of long-range anti-ship missiles and wife-guided torpedoes, FMBs are likely to become the main craft of all.

WESTERN MAIL

After being woken from a drunken sleep and asked to leave the home of his wife, a 41-year old labourer became violet and struck out.

RHYL JOURNAL AND ADVERTISER

There were only eight days during February without sin, the longest period being 7.5 hours on the 4th.

RHYL AND PRESTATYN GAZETTE

In 1996, the *Western Mail* ran a Spot-the-Ball photo which showed an item you don't normally expect to see in this kind of competition: the ball.

CRIS FREDDI

Lovely furnished modern mobile hole, select site, residential or holidays. Overlooking Aberystwyth and sea.

CAMBRIAN NEWS

MONEY

When a Cardi is deemed to be dead, a silver coin should be placed in his palm. If the fingers do not clench to grasp the coin within a minute or two, then life may be pronounced extinct with absolute safety.

TREVOR FISHLOCK *on the perceived stinginess of residents of Cardiganshire*

All capitalists should be forced to pay taxes except Welsh actors.

RICHARD BURTON

The fundamental basis of being an actor is not the desire to be the curate's son but simply to make money.

RICHARD BURTON

If I had a pound for every time people ask me, 'Don't you wish you were playing today, with the money on offer?' I would probably be a millionaire, instead of merely the millionaire they seem to think I would have become.

BARRY JOHN

There is nothing to spend money on in Talybont.

H V MORTON

The Tories have an educational system in which the most important book is the cheque book.

NEIL KINNOCK

The legend of the jungle heritage and the evolution of man as a hunting carnivore has taken root in man's mind. He may even believe that equal pay will do something terrible to his gonads.

ELAINE MORGAN

I gave Allen an unlimited budget and he exceeded it.

EDWARD WILLIAMS

Moneywise I've looked after all the men in my life.

SHIRLEY BASSEY

Compared to the jobs I used to do, snooker is money for old rope.

TERRY GRIFFITHS

75% of what I earn is spent before I see it. The money is fairy wealth.

RICHARD BURTON

I don't like charity shows. More often than not they're little more than an excuse for rich people to drink champagne. The needy get what's left.

LAURA ASHLEY

How can you say that a soccer player on £30,000 a week does a better job than a nurse or a policeman, who have to risk their lives for £14,000 a year?

NEVILLE SOUTHALL

Our ice cream man was found lying on the floor of his van covered in hundreds and thousands. The police say he topped himself.

TOMMY COOPER

Having money is rather like being a blonde. It's more fun but not vital.

MARY QUANT

Any man who has to ask about the annual upkeep of a yacht can't afford one.

J P MORGAN

I earned £2 a week in my first job as an apprentice glove-cutter.

TOM JONES

I'll do anything for money – even associate with my agent.

VINCENT PRICE

Anyone who makes a lot of money quickly must be crooked. Honest pushing away at the grindstone never made anyone a bomb.

MANDY RICE-DAVIES

In spite of all the advantages enjoyed by writers now, one feels a sort of nostalgia for the difficult old days when no one cared a damn about what one was writing and every penny one earned – if one did earn anything – came out of the pocket of the magazine editor or book publisher.

GLYN JONES

As long as people accept crap it will be financially profitable to dispense it.

DICK CAVETT

I told the Inland Revenue I didn't owe them a penny because I live near the seaside.

KEN DODD

I would have played soccer for nothing.

JOHN CHARLES

If it sells, it's art.

FRANK LLOYD WRIGHT

I got *Die Hard* because I came cheap. They were paying Bruce Willis $7 million, so they had to find people they could pay nothing.

ALAN RICKMAN

Where large sums of money are concerned, it is advisable to trust nobody.

AGATHA CHRISTIE

MOTIVATION

I have seen thousands of boys and young men, narrow-chested, hunched-up, miserable specimens, smoking endless cigarettes, many of them betting.

ROBERT BADEN-POWELL *explaining why he founded the Boy Scouts Association*

The Welsh always sang when pretending not to be scared. It kept them steady.

ROBERT GRAVES

The Welsh have been particularly fond of showing their emotions, ever since they discovered how terrified the English are of their own.

JOHN RICHARDS

I don't find it at all amusing to paint stupid millionaires when I might be painting entirely for my own satisfaction.

AUGUSTUS JOHN

The Welshman is afraid of only one thing: poverty. That is why he is kind to tramps.

CARADOC EVANS

I always do that to people I like.

VINNIE JONES *after being asked why he bit the nose of a journalist in a Dublin hotel*

Seeing *The Lost Weekend* made me teetotal – for two whole days.

HARRY SECOMBE

He always tries out his material on me and I give him constructive criticism. Why? Because I want to eat.

GWEN COOPER *on her husband Tommy*

I had a bash at positive thinking, yoga, transcendental meditation, even hypnotism. They only screwed me up, so now I'm back to my normal routine – a couple of lagers.

Darts player **LEIGHTON REES**

I've done the most unutterable rubbish all because of money. The lure of the zeros was simply too great.

RICHARD BURTON

We all thought there was more to comedy than telling jokes about mothers-in-law and a funny thing happened on the way to the theatre.

HARRY SECOMBE *on the inception of the Goons*

I sensed that most people wanted to raise families, have gardens and live life as nicely as they could. They didn't want to go out to nightclubs every night and get absolutely blotto.

LAURA ASHLEY *on the reason why she set up her traditional textile business*

I started Velvet Underground with only one ground rule: it was more important to be different than successful.

JOHN CALE

My brother didn't make it, so I have to.

DAVID JASON, *whose twin brother died at birth*

I do benefits for all religions. I'd hate to blow the hereafter on a technicality.

BOB HOPE

It was not inspiration which prompted me to start my second book, but the threadbare state of a carpet and a rattle in my car.

DICK FRANCIS

Although 'The Joshua Tree' had a lot of successful singles on it, that is not necessarily what we are about. Mind you, I need to do the roof of my house in the West, so if we get a few hits away I won't be complaining.

EDGE

MOVIES

It's in any film contract I make that the fridge in the trailer is stacked sky-high with chocolate and cakes.

DAWN FRENCH

It is hard to think of a role for which Hugh Griffith would not be too much, with his piercing glare, his insanely dominant nose, his beetling eyebrows and cavernous mouth, his over-ripe diction. God, perhaps.

DWIGHT MACDONALD

All I've seen have been a few sheep, and they've been very unenthusiastic about my new-found stardom.

SIMON WARD *after being asked how he was dealing with fame while filming 'Young Winston' outside Swansea*

I asked Julia Roberts for a date when we were filming *Notting Hill*. I figured if she married Lyle Lovett, we all had a chance.

RHYS IFANS

The first time I went to America, to promote *The Family Way*, the man from Warner Brothers called and said, 'Please spend some more money, godammit'. A couple of years later I went back to promote *Twisted Nerve*, and they were offering me drugs, chicks, booze, anything. It got so ridiculous I had to ask the film company not to send any more women around.

HYWEL BENNETT

You wouldn't know in our house whether I was a dustman or a movie star. There's no conversation about it.

VINNIE JONES

I love seeing films but I hate doing them ever since the first novelty of seeing myself on the screen wore off. I also hate the hours one has to keep. I have never been able to get up in the morning without a feeling of impending death.

IVOR NOVELLO

The cinema flattens everything into uniformity.

WYN GRIFFITH

I'd rather be unemployed than do the next script that comes in where the first thing mentioned is a frock coat.

RUFUS SEWELL

The film was untrue. I never had a love affair in my life.

Missionary **GLADYS AYLWARD** *on the depiction of her by Ingrid Bergman in 'The Inn of the Sixth Happiness'*

He would deliberately bitch up a scene if he didn't like the actors working in it.

RAY MILLAND *on the director John Farrow*

Oceans Twelve was an easier shoot than I expected. The Rat Pack left their egos at home.

CATHERINE ZETA-JONES

Films are dying of art attacks. Directors are so busy being artistic they dehydrate their simplicity. I just like to get on with it, shoot the damn thing. Too many directors stumble round looking for a needle in a haystack when it's right there under their butt end.

ANTHONY HOPKINS

When pundits foolishly aver that films have little effect on the young, I recall my own desire to swing from lamp-post to lamp-post as I made my way home along Park Street after a Tarzan epic. 'Umgawah. umgawah,' I would cry to imaginary elephants as I neared Forest Grove.

HUGH LOUDON

The only prick I've ever worked with is Nick Moran from *Lock Stock and Two Smoking Barrels*. He's got a big gob and doesn't know when to keep it shut. If he was chocolate he would have eaten himself by now.

VINNIE JONES

Black and white is a superior medium cinematically. Colour is just flat realism.

EDGE

If all the other superheroes were sitting together they'd be getting along fine with each other but they'd be thinking, 'What's wrong with that dude sitting over there?

CHRISTIAN BALE, *on Batman, whom he plays on screen*

Timothy Dalton never got a handle on James Bond. He took it too seriously. You need a hint of danger to play it right, but also the humour.

SEAN CONNERY *on the Welsh pretender to his throne*

MUSIC

The Welsh are such good singers because they have no locks on their bathroom doors.

HARRY SECOMBE

It is strange that, though they will burst into song on no provocation at all, the Welsh have produced so few eminent composers – with, of course, the exception of Johann Sebastian Bach.

ANONYMOUS

Wales has drawn more inspiration for its songs from defeat than from victory.

BEN BOWEN

When you get two Englishmen together, you get a club; two Scotsmen, a Caledonian Society; two Irishmen, a riot; and two Welshmen, a choral society.

H V MORTON

Tom Jones might have made a good light tenor if he'd practised.

STEPHEN LEWIS

Pub pianist: I hear you love music.
Dai: Yes, I do, but never mind. Keep on playing.

WYNFORD JONES

Over the years, the Treorchy Male Voice Choir has grown into something of a myth. It is said they have their own version of the wedding ceremony: 'Do you, Gladys/Glenys/Gwyneth, take this man, and also the choir?'

BYRON ROGERS

I enjoyed my schooldays very much. The only task I hated was playing the violin. It spent more time hidden in hedgerows than anywhere else.

DAI JONES

When a journalist questioned the sincerity of the Manic Street Preachers, Richey Edwards carved '4 Real' on his arm with a razor blade.

MARK LEWIS

A real Welshman would watch an all-nude ladies choir and criticise them if they sang out of tune.

GREN JONES

Much nonsense is talked about Welsh musicality, but the fact remains that, where Englishmen hum or whistle, Welshmen open their chests, square their shoulders and sing, as you can, with no sounding-board but the open air.

RONALD BRYDEN

You're either in a band in Newport or getting drunk watching a band.

JOHN SICCOLO

If we complain about the tune, there's no reason to attack the monkey when the organ grinder is present.

ANEURIN BEVAN

I wanted to be a singer as a child. I used the spout of my grand-mother's kettle as a microphone.

CATHERINE ZETA-JONES

I don't mix much with showbiz people. I hate parties because someone always traps me in a corner and asks me how I became a singer.

SHIRLEY BASSEY

The people in the cool mags don't know why the people on the street like us, and we don't either. If you think about it, your head's gonna fry.

THE STEREOPHONICS

My singing voice finished at the age of sixteen and a half. Now it's like the croak of a tired bullfrog and I would not dream of asking an audience to hear me. How much more pleasant it is to be asked, 'Why don't you sing in your shows?' than 'Why do you?'

IVOR NOVELLO

We wanted to sign to the biggest record label in the world, put out a debut album that would sell 20 million and then break up – get massive and then just throw it all away.

EDWARDS *on the deal the group signed with Sony in 1992*

We are the suicide of a non-generation.

Promotional blurb for the Preachers

I watched the Eurovision song Contest with idle ears and mobile, eyes and emerged with my misanthropy intact.

GWYN THOMAS

Charlotte Church has been all over the tabloids lately, and it's not for her beautiful renditions of light classical favourites. No, our Chari is more likely to be photographed these days falling out of a nightclub, fag in hand and propped up by her boyfriend, Gavin Henson. Since she came of age she's been on the lash, spending her copious money and generally partying for Wales.

KEVIN COURTNEY

I see the Beatles have arrived from England. They were forty pounds overweight, and that was just their hair.

BOB HOPE

We're musical primitives.

JOHN CALE *on Velvet Underground*

I've had more hit records in France than the UK. Then in Germany I have different hits again. Every time I play a different country I have to change the set to fit it.

BONNIE TYLER

The day I stop getting nervous before a recording is the day I'll stop singing.

MARY HOPKIN

I'm from a family of 13. It wasn't a rich family. I spent ten years going up and down the motorway in a tin van when I was starting out in music. We slept on floors and stopped at public conveniences to shave. Today's singers don't work their way up like that. They get thrown into talent shows too early. There's no groundwork.

SHAKIN' STEVENS

I'd like to be known as the female Elvis Presley.

SHIRLEY BASSEY

Bono is a nice bunch of guys.

U2's **THE EDGE**

The most important thing about any musician is whether he can walk into any bar and get a free drink with a song.

KEITH RICHARDS

Adolf Hitler was one of the first rock stars. Look at the way he moved. He was easily as good as Mick Jagger. He staged a country.

DAVID BOWIE

MYSTERIES

Bob Dylan says he's not a singer – so why does he sing?

TOM JONES

Who created God?

BERTRAND RUSSELL

> When are knickers panties
> and when are they briefs?
> And how do convictions differ from beliefs?
> Is an ink spot a stain or merely a blot?
> Is a monoglot Welshman Welsh or not?

PETER ELFED LEWIS

There seems to be some demand for a National Theatre in Wales. I wonder why.

LORD HOWARD DE WALDEN

We, as a people, have been around for 2000 years. Isn't it about time we got the key to our own front door?

GWYN WILLIAMS

I've always wondered why the aviation authorities don't make aeroplanes out of the same material as they use for the black box.

MAX BOYCE

If Charles is the Prince of Wales, how come he doesn't seem too upset when Wales lose to England at Twickenham?

GREN JONES

What is the metre of the dictionary?

DYLAN THOMAS

Before birds get sucked into jet engines I wonder if they ever think: Is that Rod Stewart I see in first class?'

EDDIE IZZARD

As the years go by I understand the process of producing fiction less and less. I am constantly afraid that one day I will lose the knack of it and produce discord, like a pianist forgetting where to find middle C.

DICK FRANCIS

What else do we Welsh produce but chapel ministers, actors and teachers?

ELIZABETH JAMES

Peter Brough was a huge hit when I was young. I could never understand the appeal of a ventriloquist on the radio.

JANET STREET-PORTER

If Glenn Hoddle is against the disabled, why did he pick eleven of them to play for England?

IAN HISLOP

I was once accused wrongly of being a thief and it almost wrecked my life. How much worse must it have been for you to have been accused of a terrible thing that was true?

RICHARD MADELEY *to Bill Clinton regarding the Monica Lewinsky affair*

Musically we tend not to give in to logic any more. Mystery gives the tempo, the emotion and the setting.

EDGE *on U2*

NAMES

My real name is Michael Barratt. My nickname didn't come from my singing style. It came from the way I used to stand at the wicket as a schoolboy cricketer.

SHAKIN' STEVENS

London bastards changed the Welsh counties about, and then gave them all those crappy ancient names.

KINGSLEY AMIS

My real name is Reginald Alfred John Truscott-Jones. When I first arrived in Hollywood they told me to get a new one. I thought back to the times I had as a kid in Wales. There was a tannery and old mills. It was really 'mill land'. So I called myself Jack Milland. But they said, 'In Hollywood, only dogs are called Jack.' So I looked down a list and picked the shortest name I could find – Ray.

RAY MILLAND

An Englishman in Wales sees a factory called Jones Manufacturing Company and muses, 'So that's where they make them.'

TREVOR FISHLOCK

The Welsh are insistent that Welsh names must not be pronounced as they are spelt.

JOHN TICKNER

Hard men in football? Well, there was that picture of Vinnie Jones holding Gazza's wotsits. In my day, we called someone who did that a poof.

GEORGE BEST

Broadcasters make brave tries at Russian and Arabic titles, but give a laugh and a shrug at simple names like Ynysybwl or Pwllheli.

MICHAEL ASPEL

My full name is Thomas George Thomas. In Wales, such duplication invariably leads to the nickname Tommy Twice.

GEORGE THOMAS

There's a restaurant in Tokyo run by a Welshwoman named Jane Best Cook. She was Jane Cook and she married a guy named Best.

PAMELA PETRO

PEOPLE AND PLACES

Anglesey is one enormous farm.

H V MORTON

Many of Wales' early rugby players and administrators at club and international level were neither Welsh by birth nor by language. Many were Welsh only through the aspiration to play for Wales.

DAI SMITH

We in Swansea are Welsh by birth, but not Welsh-speaking or Welsh-thinking.

ELIZABETH JAMES

Everybody goes into the pub sideways, and the dogs piss only on back doors, and there are more unwanted babies shoved up the chimneys than there are used French letters in the offertory boxes.

DYLAN THOMAS *on Llangain in 1944*

Nobody knows for certain how many groups there are in Newport. It is probably possible to go deaf quicker here than on the Western Front.

BYRON ROGERS

A visitor to homes in Glamorgan is asked to help himself to sugar for his tea. In Carmarthenshire, he is asked whether he wants one lump or two. But in Carmarthenshire, they say, 'Are you sure you stirred it?'

HUW WILLIAMS

Wales is where the boy I was and the man I am not met, hesitated, left double footsteps, then walked on.

DANNIE ABSE

In Laugharne you have a town of almost defiant calmness.

GWYN THOMAS

There are those who would question the sanity of one who voluntarily spends a long weekend in Swansea.

ANON

If Borth is the poor man's Aberystwyth – and it isn't – then Clarach is the poor man's Borth. And that's about as poor as you can get without selling a kidney. It's not a one-horse town, not even a hoof – maybe the imprint left by a horseshoe nailed once long ago to a fence, or maybe just a handful of oats.

MALCOLM PRYCE

There is something sadistic about a Sunday in Aberystwyth.

RHYS DAVIES

I was born in Holyhead, the home town of Harry Secombe. I was also given his legs.

DAWN FRENCH

Only friends could bring me again to Swansea. The town is a dirty witch. You must hate or love her – and I both hate and love her.

EDWARD THOMAS

All there is in Laugharne is rain, torpor and Ivy's dungeon.

DYLAN THOMAS

I once went to a party in Haverfordwest on a Thursday evening. It finished in Hungary the following Tuesday.

AUGUSTUS JOHN

I would feel more at home in Madras than in Machynlleth.

ROY JENKINS

Aberystwyth is the perfect town for the unambitious man.

WYNFORD VAUGHAN-THOMAS

Aberystwyth to a Birmingham man suggests bathing, boating and a day out at the Devil's Bridge, but to a Welshman it is the town where Blodwen is trying to be a teacher and where David is climbing out of the agricultural into the professional classes.

H V MORTON

Cardiffians think West Wales means Penarth.

GREN JONES

In the nineteenth century, Carmarthen had more pubs and murders than Dodge City.

BYRON ROGERS

POETRY AND POETS

A poet's task is not to criticise life but to explain it. When he turns to criticism he is no longer a poet.

JOHN JENKINS

> Poets of Wales, like trees of fire
> Light the black twentieth century.

ADRIAN MITCHELL

Wales bred two poets of great renown in the English-speaking world, both called Thomas. They're easy to tell apart. Dylan was the Thomas who sometimes wrote nonsense when under the influence of alcohol, while R S Thomas was the Thomas who sometimes talked nonsense when stone cold sober.

JOHN RICHARDS

The only nice poets I've ever met were bad ones. A bad poet is not a poet at all. Ergo, I've never met a nice poet.

RICHARD BURTON

Poets get off to a rugged start. There is no field of art in which so much pure intelligence is going to be expended for so little return. Indeed, I can see the day when inbred potencies are listed and charted at birth. Those in danger of a tumble with the muse will be given an instant shot of whatever hormones make a man a satisfied fairground barker.

GWYN THOMAS

The poetry that makes nothing happen is something we cannot afford.

HARRI WEBB

Never trust a poet who can drive. If he can drive, distrust the poems.

MARTIN AMIS

Poetry is the only lost cause we've got left. It fights for the impossible.

JOHN COWPER POWYS

I do not know how to write a poem. If I did, I wouldn't be able to write one.

DANNIE ABSE

Poetry is sissy stuff that rhymes.

GEOFFREY WILLIAMS

Wales is a land of poets – but it's the poets who say that.

T E NICHOLAS

POLITICS

As long as there is food and drink and greyhounds and cinemas, the majority of our people do not care what government is in power.

R S THOMAS

Is the Welsh political genius to have no future expression except in a miserable parish pump assembly at Cardiff?

LEO ABSE *on devolution in 1979*

All Celtic people are, at heart, Communists.

KEIR HARDIE

Prime Ministers tend to be either bookmakers or bishops.

JAMES CALLAGHAN

There was a break-in at the West Glamorgan council offices, and the chairman was interviewed the following morning by a reporter from BBC Wales. He asked if there was anything of value stolen. 'Yes,' replied the chairman, 'the results of next month's elections.'

WYNFORD JONES

If Wales is to be governed by a nation outside our land, I would prefer it to be from Dublin.

GWYNFOR EVANS

I am so little eager for an independent Wales that I would as soon re-establish Druidism in Anglesey as set up an independent parliament in Caernarfon.

HENRY JONES

The road to a Welsh hell will be paved with the good intentions of Labour's devolutionists.

TIM WILLIAMS

Looking at the state of democracy in Britain today reminds me of the man of eighty who, when asked how he felt now that he had reached such an age, replied, 'Very well, especially when I consider the alternative.'

GEORGE THOMAS

POLITICAL INVECTIVE

If we could adapt Horace Walpole's wry view of human existence and say politics is a comedy to those who think and a tragedy to those who feel, we have the best description of devolution so far.

GWYN JONES

I have only three words to say about Welsh Nationalism, and two of them are 'Welsh Nationalism'.

DYLAN THOMAS

Of course you hate choice. You are a socialist, a crypto-Communist.

MARGARET THATCHER *to Neil Kinnock in 1990*

David Lloyd George can't see a belt without hitting below it.

MARGOT ASQUITH

As Moses, James Callaghan would have mistimed his arrival at the parting of the waters.

AUSTIN MITCHELL

If you want Margaret Thatcher to change her mind you don't use argument. You look for a transplant surgeon.

JOHN EDMONDS

I can still remember the day when I encountered my first Conservative, a shock all the greater in that it coincided with the crisis of puberty.

GWYN WILLIAMS

The Welsh expect their politicians to be corrupt or incompetent or both. They are rarely disappointed.

JOHN RICHARDS

Home Rule for Ireland? Yes. And Home Rule for Scotland? Why not. Home Rule for Wales? Certainly. And Home Rule even for England!

DAVID LLOYD GEORGE

George Bush's carefully thought out policy towards Iraq is the only way to bring about international peace and security. The one certain way to stop Muslim fundamentalist suicide bombers targeting the US and the UK is to bomb a few Muslim countries that have never threatened us.

IAN HISLOP

Neil Kinnock has an infallible knack for getting the wrong end of every stick.

SIR CYRIL SMITH

Tony Blair has done more U-Turns than a dodgy plumber.

IAIN DUNCAN SMITH

No one can be against Michael Heseltine and be all bad.

EDWARD PEARCE

A First Minister whose self-righteous stubbornness has not been equalled, save briefly by Neville Chamberlain, since Lord North.

ROY JENKINS *on Margaret Thatcher*

James Callaghan is living proof that the short term schemer and the frustrated bully can be made manifest in one man.

HUGO YOUNG

George Washington never told a lie. I don't know how he ever made it in politics.

BOB HOPE

Bill Clinton didn't tell Monica Lewinsky to lie. He told her to *kneel*.

IAN HISLOP

There's nobody in politics I can remember where a man combined such a powerful political personality with so little intelligence.

ROY JENKINS *on James Callaghan*

You can say what you like about Kinnock, but God help you if you say what you don't like.

NATALIE UPTON

The self-appointed king of the gutter of politics.

MICHAEL HESELTINE *on Neil Kinnock*

He aroused every feeling except trust.

A J P TAYLOR ON LLOYD GEORGE

Aneurin Bevan's first act under the new National Health Service should be to find its best psychiatrist and get himself treated.

WINSTON CHURCHILL

PREDICTIONS

I'd said we would win, but your talent overwhelmed my mind.

URI GELLER *to Ryan Giggs, after Manchester United beat Geller's Reading in the FA Cup in 1990*

I daresay I will go on writing books until I can't.

DICK FRANCIS

My guess is that the last World War will be fought between the literate and the vandalistic mob. The cause of the war might well be a decision to repeat 'Match of the Day' on all channels right through the week.

GWYN THOMAS

He enjoys prophesying the imminent fall of the capitalist system and is prepared to play a part, any part, in its burial except that of a mute.

HAROLD MACMILLAN *on Aneurin Bevan*

When Paramount made *The Lost Weekend* and the studio heads first saw it, they came to the conclusion that what they had seen was a well-made, socially conscious documentary that would lay an ostrich egg.

RAY MILLAND *on the movie that ended up winning him an Oscar*

I am told that in the not too distant future we will all be able to read our own medical records on the internet. For entertainment, I think I'll stick to *Coronation Street*.

AELWYN ROBERTS

If Margaret Thatcher is re-elected, I warn you not to be ordinary, I warn you not to be young, I warn you not to fall ill, and I warn you not to grow old.

NEIL KINNOCK IN 1983

If she dies before I do, I'll turn into a tyre on a bus and roll forever and forever over innocent feet.

RICHARD BURTON *on his devotion to Elizabeth Taylor*

I'll keep swivelling my hips until they need replacing.

TOM JONES

One day, when Wales is free and prosperous
And dull, they'll all be wishing they were us.

HARRI WEBB

When I take up assassination, I shall start with the surgeons and work up to the gutter.

DYLAN THOMAS

Aneurin Bevan will be a curse to this country in peace just as he was a squalid nuisance in time of war.

WINSTON CHURCHILL

PUNS

Wales is very sparsely copulated.

SIR ALEC DOUGLAS HOME

A customer walked into a Swansea bar. 'Bitter?' asked the barman. 'No,' the customer replied, 'just very, very sad.'

WYNFORD JONES

Middle age is when your age starts to show around the middle.

BOB HOPE

Agatha Christie has given more pleasure in bed than any other woman in history.

NANCY BANKS-SMITH

Did you hear about the new satire on social mores? It's called 'How Green was my Valet.'

SYLVIA ROBERTS

My family ate nothing but 'poached' salmon.

RICHARD BURTON

Sodom and Begorrah.

DYLAN THOMAS *on Samuel Beckett's 'Murphy'*

There's something Vichy about the French.

IVOR NOVELLO

Did you hear about the two TV aerials that got married? The ceremony was rubbish but the reception was brilliant.

TOMMY COOPER

My teeth are my own – I paid for them.

KEN DODD

Too many cocks spoil the breath.

DYLAN THOMAS

Some people have told me I should have been hung instead of my pictures.

AUGUSTUS JOHN

As we drove to the training grounds, we noticed that the further out we went towards the townships, the more startling the change in housing, roads and general conditions became. It was, literally and metaphorically, black and white.

BARRY JOHN *on playing rugby in South Africa under apartheid*

Could a female director be called a broad-caster?

HUW ELLIS

Maybe Charlotte Church should now be called Charlotte Club.

BRYONY LEWIS

He's got a photographic mind. It's a pity it never developed.

HYWEL ROBERTS

RELIGION

A Welshman is a man who prays on his knees on Sunday and preys on his friends the rest of the week.

ENGLISH SAYING

God first made England, Ireland and Scotland. Then, when he corrected his mistakes, he made Wales.

KATHARINE HEPBURN

Wales is a land of great religious density, but deplorably short of baths and hairdressers.

J PARRY LEWIS

The great mistake of Welsh literature in our time is that we have no anti-Christian writers. We only have heretics.

SAUNDERS LEWIS

Dylan Thomas was a religious poet.

VERNON WATKINS

A healthy paganism would heal many of Wales' maladies.

H IDRIS BELL

A living paganism is much nearer to heaven than a dead religion.

D J WILLIAMS

My father came from Welsh stock. One of his most vivid memories as a little boy was listening to his kneeling grandfather rehearse an address for the weekly prayer meeting. Puzzled as to who was being spoken to in such a loud voice, he was told that his grandfather was 'in touch with God'.

MICHAEL YORK

REPARTEE

Negotiating with Eamon De Valera is like trying to pick up mercury with a fork.

>*Remark attributed to* **DAVID LLOYD GEORGE.** *De Valera is alleged to have replied, 'Then why doesn't he use a spoon?'*

A woman went to the doctor and told him that every morning she found herself singing 'Delilah' and every night, 'The Green, Green Grass of Home'. 'That's called the Tom Jones Syndrome,' the doctor informed her. 'Is it rare?' she enquired. 'It's not unusual,' he said.

>**HUW ELLIS**

On the water, I presume?

>**DAVID LLOYD GEORGE** *after being informed by Lord Beaverbrook's butler that he was out walking.*

Don't worry. The Welsh are really Irishmen – just Protestants.

>*Film director* **JOHN FORD** *to Irish screenwriter Philip Dunne on the set of* How Green was my Valley. *Dunne was leery about adapting Richard Llewellyn's famous novel because he had never set foot in Wales.*

By wearing tin drawers.

>**DYLAN THOMAS** *when he was asked how a woman could best preserve her honour under a Communist regime.*

In one hotel, after noticing they had lamb on the menu, I innocently asked the waiter, 'Is it Welsh?' He replied curtly, 'Do you want to eat it or talk to it?

>**MAX BOYCE**

Mark Harcombe used to tell of a man who called at the Naval Colliery in Penygraig to look for work. The manager said sharply, 'You know there's nothing for you here. Come back in the spring.' Instantly the reply came, 'What do you think I am – a bloody cuckoo?'

GEORGE THOMAS

That's nothing. Only yesterday we had a vicar in *The Sun*.

JAC Y WYDDOR *to an American who boasted that his country had a man on the moon*

REVULSION

The earth contains no race of human beings so totally vile and worthless as the Welsh. I have expended in labour, within three years, nearly £8000 amongst them, and yet they treat me as their greatest enemy.

WALTER SAVAGE LANDOR

I want Wales to lose every game, so that the manager might be sacked. We're the Man. City of international football. We rank 98th in the world, below the Congo Republic.

NICKY WIRE *in 1998*

Welsh Labour Councillors are all the same. They're short, they're fat, and they're fundamentally corrupt.

ROD RICHARDS

He really is a smugly pompous little bastard and is cavalier about everybody except Black Panthers and Indians.

RICHARD BURTON *on Marlon Brando*

Vinnie Jones is a player who regards it as a matter of personal honour to intimidate the nation's finest, to castrate them with a shattering late tackle early in the game, to rip their ears off and spit in the hole.

JASPER REES

If I was in the gutter, which I ain't, he'd still be looking up at me from the sewer.

NEIL KINNOCK *on Michael Heseltine*

Every time I hear Tom Jones I want to jump out of a window.

SCOTT WALKER

An honest Welshman is not a miracle. The miracle is how he became honest.

CARADOC EVANS

Shirley MacLaine is the most obnoxious actress I've ever worked with.

ANTHONY HOPKINS

Rolf Harris is a difficult man to hate, but that doesn't mean we shouldn't try.

A A GILL

I couldn't warm to Chuck Berry even if I was cremated next to him.

KEITH RICHARDS

I wouldn't sit on Joan Crawford's toilet.

BETTE DAVIS

ROYALTY

I'm prepared to take advice on leisure from Prince Philip. He's a world expert on it, having been practising it for most of his life.

NEIL KINNOCK

The Princess of Wails.

DILWYN JONES' *view of Princess Diana when she started speaking out against her alienated husband*

One day, exhausted after a night shift and desperate for sleep, a miner went to his bed after instructing his wife he wasn't to be disturbed on any account. He hadn't drifted long into sleep when she burst into the room. 'Evan, Evan,' she cried, shaking him vigorously, 'The king is dead.' He opened one eye. 'Thank God it's only that,' he said, turning over. 'I thought the coal was being delivered.'

TREVOR FISHLOCK

The life of one Welsh miner is of greater commercial and moral value than the whole royal crowd put together.

KEIR HARDIE

At the FA Cup Final in 1961 the Queen asked Danny Blanchflower why the Tottenham players didn't have their names emblazoned on their shirts. 'Well you see, ma'am,' he told her, 'all our players know each other.'

BARRY JOHN

Ian Hislop looks rather like King Edward – the potato, not the monarch.

PAUL MERTON

Anyone standing to attention for 'God Save the Queen' at a film nowadays is either the producer of the little film of Her Majesty that goes with it, or he's inadvertently tied his shoelaces together.

HARRY SECOMBE

I've danced with a man who's danced with a girl who's danced with the Prince of Wales.

HERBERT FARJEON

I left England when I was four because I found out I couldn't be king.

BOB HOPE

After his coronation, King Farouk didn't read a single book. He glanced through the State papers during short spells in the toilet, and probably signified assent or rejection by a system of coded rattles on the chain.

GWYN THOMAS

For quite a while during my childhood I held the romantic notion that I was really a royal prince. I used to search my person for anything resembling a birthmark, a mole, or a wart even, that would reveal to me my true identity. The best I could come up with was a blind boil, which I discovered on the back of my neck, by arranging the mirrors on the dressing table.

HARRY SECOMBE

Reasonable behaviour on the part of royalty or celebrities is translated into wonderful behaviour; the expectation is much less, I suppose.

SIAN PHILLIPS

RUGBY

In 1823, William Webb Ellis first picked up the ball in his arms and ran with it. And for the next 156 years forwards have been trying to work out why.

SIR TASKER WATKINS

The English rugby team? I've seen better centres in a box of Black Magic.

MAX BOYCE

Wales didn't even have enough imagination to thump someone in the line-out when the ref wasn't looking.

J P R WILLIAMS

We decided on a new strategy in the Welsh pack. A word sign beginning with the letter P was the signal to go forward to the right. When, predictably, Gareth Edwards called, 'Psychology,' half the forwards went left.

CARWYN JONES *on silent letters*

These days you have to be able to concentrate for an hour non-stop. You're drenched in perspiration – and that's just *Panorama*.

WILL CARLING

The reason Welsh rugby players haven't any teeth is to stop them biting each other.

MAX BOYCE

We lost seven of our last eight matches. The only team we beat is Western Samoa. It's just as well we didn't have to play the whole of Samoa.

GARETH DAVIES

I knew he would never play for Wales – he's tone deaf.

VERNON DAVIES *after his son Huw opted to play rugby for England*

In his search for a ticket to an international match at Cardiff Arms Park, a Welshman becomes as commercial as an opium dealer, as heartless as a highwayman, as cunning as a cat. This normally generous man, who would give you the lamb chop from his plate, would exhume his grandfather if he thought there was one accidentally folded into the shroud.

TREVOR FISHLOCK

Rugby apart, the Welsh only seem dimly aware of the rest of the planet.

JOHN RICHARDS

You can never beat the Welsh. You can only score more points.

GRAHAM MOURIE

I remember the first time I played for Wales. I was nine. It was against England in Llewellyn Street. We had 28 on our side and they had eleven on theirs. It wasn't fair but it was my ball. We won 406 to 212. I scored 23 tries before I was carried off injured. I was late tackling the touchline, three yards short of my anorak. We went on to beat Scotland and Ireland before 3 o'clock. We would have beaten France as well, but Jack Edgar kicked the ball into Mrs. Edwards' garden and she wouldn't let us have it back.

MAX BOYCE

You enjoy rugby more if you don't know the rules. Also, it puts you on the same wavelength as the referees.

GARETH DAVIES

Cosmeticised and fineried, she looks less like a Welsh whore than part of a deal that included Richard Burton.

STANLEY KAUFFMANN *on Liz Taylor in* Under Milk Wood

What do you gargle with – pebbles?

PRINCE PHILIP TO TOM JONES

In general, North Walians and South Walians get on like a house on fire, the house in question having been bought by a South Walian and set on fire by a North Walian.

JOHN RICHARDS

Your pace is very deceptive, son. You're even slower than you look.

ALEX FERGUSON *to Leighton James*

Shout, 'Yes,' in a Welsh street and a dozen people will shout back, 'No.'

DAI WATKINS

My father always said he was the fittest caddie in a tournament because he had to walk further than anyone else when he carried my bag.

IAN WOOSNAM

She's a nice fat girl who loves mosquitoes and hates pustular, carbuncular Welshmen, loathes boats and loves planes, has tiny blackcurrant eyes and minute breasts, and has no sense of humour.

RICHARD BURTON *on Liz Taylor*

If the Welsh only knew more philosophy, what brilliant philosophers they'd make.

DAI EVANS

These days I see rugby players at the highest level becoming a combination of 200-metre runners, javelin-throwers and pole-vaulters.

BARRY JOHN

Richard Burton, Welsh Actor, Tax-Free Switzerland.

Address on a letter once received by Burton. He took the jibe in good faith

SCHOOL

Gomer Jenkins was the principal of my primary school in Wales. He sometimes used the cane on us, but most often his fists. To this day, no amateur can hurt me with a right hook due to my constant study of Gomer's feet.

RAY MILLAND

The little Welsh history taught in schools in my day was merely an appendix to the history of England, the story of a conquered province from which all colour and light had been drained under the deep shadow of its conqueror.

GWYNFOR EVANS

I learnt more on my way to and from school than I ever did in the classroom.

DAI JONES

My father wanted me to have all the educational opportunities he never had, so he sent me to a girl's school.

KEN DODD

How to survive in boarding school: Do not express emotion. Do not have emotion. If someone hits you, hit them back. If someone argues with you, argue back. Never give an inch, never look vulnerable.

EDDIE IZZARD

Gillian Anderson always reminds me of a supply teacher.

DAVID BADDIEL

What do you say to a successful graduate with a first class degree? 'I'll have a Big Mac, please.'

DANNIE ABSE

He was sent to a public school, where a little learning was painfully beaten into him, and from thence to the university, where it was carefully taken out again.

THOMAS LOVE PEACOCK

If Harold Wilson ever went to school without any boots, it was because he was too big for them.

IVOR BULMER-THOMAS

Our classrooms reek of dead and wasted talents.

GWYN THOMAS

School for me was mainly a social event. I was never very interested in exams.

GAVIN HENSON

My favourite occupation at school was dodging games. In those days, there were no tracksuits for girls. You had to put on stupid short skirts to play hockey in the freezing cold.

CAROL VORDERMAN

In Wales, history in school has nearly always meant English history.

TREVOR FISHLOCK

Schoolmasters are eternal optimists, always hoping to spot a thoroughbred among the donkeys.

PAUL FERRIS

Unless you have been to boarding school when you are very young, it is absolutely impossible to appreciate the delights of living at home.

ROALD DAHL

School for me was an intolerable interruption of the serious business of life. Father did not care whether I went or not, so it was entirely due to mother's firmness that I attended at all. Employing some determination and a lot of guile, however, I managed to average only three days a week.

DICK FRANCIS

Poor Elizabeth. She was educated at MGM.

RICHARD BURTON *on Liz Taylor's unfortunate fate*

As late as 1960, it was possible to meet old people who remembered nothing of their schooldays except the learning by rote of a book known to them as 'Redimarisi' – 'Reading Made Easy'.

JOHN DAVIES

The teacher who kicks away his pedestal steps on to a gallows. The one who thinks an unremitting mateyness and familiarity are the keys to his pupils' hearts will soon find himself in schools where Tarzan swings in for his annual trip of inspection.

GWYN THOMAS

Lessons interrupted games.

JOHN CHARLES

SELF-CRITICISM

When Freud met Einstein they got on famously. Freud reported, 'Einstein understands as much about psychology as I do about physics, so we had a very pleasant talk.'

DANNIE ABSE

Sometimes I play snooker like a pig with a shotgun.

MARK WILLIAMS

I like the word 'indolence'. It makes my laziness sound classy.

BERN WILLIAMS

Always for me there's been that niggling feeling that I was being an emotional prostitute.

RAY MILLAND

I'd shoot myself if I had the bottle.

VINNIE JONES *after being sent off for the tenth time during the 1995 soccer season*

I wouldn't know a painting from a cowpat.

AUGUSTUS JOHN

I want everything yesterday.

ANTHONY HOPKINS

I've just been voted women's favourite role model in a magazine poll. I demand a recount.

DAWN FRENCH

Please excuse my English. I learned it in Wormwood Scrubs.

D J WILLIAMS

I write English like a dead language.

BOBI JONES

I used to frighten the life out of my opponents in my boxing days – by bleeding all over them. I spent so much time on the canvas, my nickname was Rembrandt. I made a fortune by selling advertising on the soles of my feet.

TOMMY COOPER

I have this terrible fear that I'm going to be forced to take a general knowledge test in public.

DICK CAVETT

My life has been one long descent into respectability.

MANDY RICE-DAVIES

Like all ignorant Englishmen, I believed Cardiff would have coal-mines in the main street.

MICHAEL ASPEL

I'm a Welsh dwarf and it's always been my fate to be cast with tall leading ladies.

RICHARD BURTON *to Louise Fletcher on the set of 'The Heretic'*

I can't run, can't pass, can't tackle, can't shoot, but I'm still here.
VINNIE JONES *In 1997*

I sometimes feel that I'm impersonating the dark unconscious of the human race. I know that sounds sick, but I love it.
VINCENT PRICE

I'm not an innovator. I'm really just a Photostat machine.
DAVID BOWIE

I do not mock hypochondriacs, however often they put out their tongues at the mirror or stare with peculiar sadness at their own faeces in the lavatory bowl. I was once a medical student, and all medical students become temporary hypochondriacs.
DANNIE ABSE

I'm an instant star. Just add water and stir.
DAVID BOWIE

I am humble enough to recognise that I have made mistakes, but politically astute enough to have forgotten what they are.
MICHAEL HESELTINE

We have become the sort of people our parents warned us about.
AUGUSTUS JOHN *to Nina Hamnett*

I must be the only Welshman ever born tone deaf.
EMLYN WILLIAMS

I've done as much for golf as Truman Capote has for Sumo wrestling.

BOB HOPE

I'm a sausage machine.

AGATHA CHRISTIE

Perhaps because I have concentrated harder than most on my own exploits – a very Welsh trait, it has made me narrow-minded, or at least to appear so. In my heart I hate a narrow attitude but often one hates most in others those faults in one's own character one is struggling to overcome.

LAURA ASHLEY

My handwriting has been a constant source of strain for devoted secretaries who have struggled to interpret my illegible scrawl over many years. I strongly suspect this started as a deliberate cover-up through which I learned to hide my inability to spell.

MICHAEL HESELTINE

I've made more than eighty films and all but five of them have been bad.

STANLEY BAKER

I lurch from indecision to indecision. All I ever seem to do is smash up against my own limitations.

ALAN RICKMAN

Mobile phones are the only subject on which men boast about who's got the smallest.

NEIL KINNOCK

There's no Welsh word for orgasm, but I know a very good one for adulterer.

MAIR GRIFFITHS

What's the difference between the Irish and the Welsh? Sex. The Irish prefer women to drink. The pleasure the Welsh find in drink is in addition to, and not a substitute for, bed.

DONALD BAVERSTOCK

The Welsh are obsessed with sheep lust, both real and imagined. One man, caught in a compromising position with one of his livestock, actually swore in court that he was peeing in a field when a sheep backed up on to his penis.

PAMELA PETRO

Getting pregnant was the worst thing that could befall a girl in the 1950s. We were threatened with a lifetime behind the counter at Woolworth's. The young men knew their contribution towards such a fate ensured that they would become providers, working at the most boring jobs imaginable while remaining chained in a dutiful and probably loveless marriage.

SIAN PHILLIPS

The first time I had sex with Michael Hutchence, he did six things with me that I'm sure were illegal.

PAULA YATES

All the adaptations I saw of *Pride and Prejudice* had people in stiff suits standing up very straight and making polite conversation through pursed lips in drawing-rooms. But I felt the story was more about young men and women in the prime of their lives, with lots of hormones pounding around.

ANDREW DAVIES

The more a girl covers herself up, the more sexual she is.

LAURA ASHIEY

If there's anything I don't want to wear, or a photographer is getting too raunchy, I'm like, 'Whoa there, fella. I'm not a Page 3 girl.' But, unfortunately, sex sells. It's fine to be sexy but there's a thin line between sexy and sexual.

CHARLOTTE CHURCH *on her revamped image*

Gazza said that scoring was better than an orgasm. Lee Chapman reckoned it wasn't as good. I'll go with Pele – he thought it was about the same.

RYAN GIGGS

To stop lusting is to die.

SAUNDERS LEWIS

Transsexuals always seem to feel they have Shirley Bassey trapped inside their bodies instead of an assistant from an Oxfam shop.

PAUL HOGGART

My wife doesn't. Understand me?

THOMAS HUMPHREYS

I'm a lesbian trapped in a man's body.

EDDIE IZZARD

He never washed anything so the kitchen was awful. It was the right background for our experiments in sex.

MARY QUANT

I'm a believer in safe sex. I put a handrail round the bed.

KEN DODD

SNOOKER

I knew things couldn't be going too well when I saw the organiser in a gorilla suit, going up and down the prom selling tickets.

Ex-snooker pro **DOUG MOUNTJOY** on an exhibition match he played once in Rhyl

The colour of the snooker table fascinates me. Having an allergy to lawn mowers, I find a deep calm in the sight of anything green that doesn't grow.

GWYN THOMAS

He uses running side, reverse side, back side, any sort of side. The only side he hasn't attempted is suicide.

RAY REARDON on Alex Higgins. Actually Higgins did attempt the latter as well, according to his autobiography

I hope Barry Hearn doesn't go out of snooker because the only other job he would want is God's and that will take a bit of getting.

CLIFF WILSON

He's a bit of a Jekyll and Hyde character with me. One minute he says hello, the next he's blanking me.

RONNIE O'SULLIVAN on Mark Williams

Stupid people say stupid things.

WILLIAMS *in response to the previous quotation*

A gentle Welsh dragon.

RAY REARDON *on Doug Mountjoy*

I used to be a civil servant. Government cutbacks meant I had to go into snooker full time. Talk about a blessing in disguise.

REFEREE JOHN WILLIAMS

So important is Terry Griffiths' hairstyle that it now has its own management contract and has, in the past, demanded equal appearance money with Terry.

GEOFF ATKINSON

The best single ball potter in the world.

WILLIE THORNE *on Mark Williams*

He's held substantial leads in two world finals now and managed to lose both. That has to play on your mind a bit.

PHIL YATES *on Matthew Stevens*

I agree with the man who described snooker as chess with balls.

ANTHONY DAVIES

Ray very very rarely bites anyone. In fact, I personally have only been bitten by him three times, and the last time I wouldn't even have noticed if he hadn't leapt on my back and started to claw at my neck.

STEVE DAVIS *joking about Ray Reardon's 'Dracula' soubriquet*

SPORT

At the school sports I flattened so many hurdles they abolished the event and switched me to the marathon, where I was reported lost for a week.

GWYN THOMAS

The triple jump is only jumping into a sandpit.

JONATHAN EDWARDS

The only thing I have against golf is that it takes you so far from the clubhouse.

ERIC LINKLATER

When I step off the plane at a tournament venue, I go to the hotel and relax with friends. When Tiger Woods steps off a plane, he goes to the treadmill.

IAN WOOSNAM

I once got into the ring with Muhammad Ali. I had him worried for a while. He thought he'd killed me.

TOMMY COOPER

My cue is an extension of my right arm.

RAY REARDON

A good darts player who can count can always beat a brilliant one who can't.

LEIGHTON REES

I need six or seven pints and a half dozen trips to the gents before I'm ready to play darts.

ALUN EVANS

You get to know more of the character of a man in a round of golf than you can get to know in six months with only political experience.

DAVID LLOYD GEORGE

I only have to read Joe Louis' name and my nose starts to bleed again.

TOMMY FARR

THEATRE

I wrote *Jackie the Jumper* because I wanted to write a play that painted the full face of sensuality, rebellion and revivalism. In south Wales, these three phenomena have played second fiddle only to the Rugby Union, which is a distillation of all three.

GWYN THOMAS

Ah, Victor, still struggling to keep your head below water!

EMLYN WILLIAMS *to fellow actor Victor Spinetti*

Between you and me, I am not all that much of a better dramatist than Sophocles.

SAUNDERS LEWIS

Wales is the only country in the world where television came before theatre.

WILBERT LLOYD ROBERTS

A trumpet blares and on to the stage struts Richard Burton as Hamlet. But he only looks like a film-star with the sulks.

JOHN BARBER

Acting is somehow shameful for a man to do. It isn't natural to put on make-up and wear costumes on stage and say someone else's lines. So you drink to overcome the shame.

RICHARD BURTON

During a love scene played by Emrys Jones and Mary Mackenzie, a dog cocked his leg against the sofa they were sitting on and peed endlessly. The pee ran down the footlights, which immediately fused, and went off like a series of firecrackers.

BRYAN FORBES *on (mis)directing* Gathering Storm *at the beginning of his career.*

She interprets the heroine as if she were Richard Crookback under a dose of Novocaine. Hunching her back and moodily surveying the floorboards, she balefully drags out her funniest lines as if they were a defeated political candidate's good wishes to the winner.

JOHN SIMON *on Rachel Roberts in* The Visit

DYLAN THOMAS ON HIMSELF

I have achieved poverty with distinction, but never poverty with dignity. The best I can manage is dignity with poverty. I would sooner smarm like a fart-licking spaniel than starve in a world of fat bones.

When I am a rich man, with my own bicycle, and can have beer for breakfast, I shall give up writing poetry altogether.

I fell in love with words at once, and am still at their mercy. But, I have also learned to beat them now and then, which they appear to enjoy.

My mind is like a Welsh railway – one track and dirty.

The fact that I'm unemployed helps to add to my natural hatred of Wales.

DYLAN THOMAS ON POETRY

I hate the hushed voice and hats-off attitude to poetry.

The Welsh have written exceedingly good poetry in English. I like to think that is because they were good poets rather than good Welshmen.

Too many of the artists of Wales spend too much time talking about the position of the artists of Wales. There is only one position for an artist anywhere: upright.

A poet's middle leg is his phallic pencil. If it turns into a pneumatic drill, breaking up the tar and the concrete of language worn thin by the tricycle tyres of nature poets, and the heavy six wheels of the academic sirs, so much the better.

If you want a definition of poetry, say, 'It's what makes me laugh or cry or yawn, what makes my toenails twinkle, what makes me want to do this or that or nothing.'

Poetry is not the most important thing in life. I'd much rather lie in a hot bath, reading Agatha Christie and sucking sweets.

OTHERS ON DYLAN THOMAS

He grappled with life as if it were a policeman.
CHRISTOPHER ISHERWOOD

He drank his own blood and ate his own marrow to get the material for his poetry.

THEODORE ROETHKE

Dylan was at core a typical Welsh Puritan and Nonconformist gone wrong.

AUGUSTUS JOHN

To the horror of a few die-hard nationalists, he became, with the inexorable logic of the MTV generation, a symbol of modern Welsh culture.

ANDREW LYCETT

He reminds me of those fake, nostalgic, bourgeois reincarnations of boyhood of some compatriots who've never really lived intensely, or felt. A teashop gossip, a beauty at a remove.

KEIDRICH RHYS

Had he lived twenty years in an igloo with the Eskimos, he would never have become an Eskimo in an igloo. He would always have been Dylan.

CAITLIN THOMAS

TRAVEL

When going abroad, get yourself a decent hamper from Fortnum and Mason's and keep away from the native women.

EDWARD EVANS

The traveller in Wales cannot fail to be struck by two things: the romantic beauty of the country and the absolute lack of romance exhibited by the people.

T W CROSLAND

More and more Welsh signs lead to fewer and fewer Welsh places.

NED THOMAS

In Blaenau, it was the three-speed gear that separated the sheep from the goats.

AELWYN ROBERTS

It's great to be back on terra cotta.

JOHN PRESCOTT *after a lengthy trip*

In the 1930s, when we lived in Cardiff, our car seemed to know only one route. It would go instinctively to Ogmore-by-the-sea.

DANNIE ABSE

The Aberystwyth Cliff Railway is the train you take when your life has gone wrong. It creeps up the hill at the speed of lichen. You get off at the top, fortify yourself from a Styrofoam cup with tea the colour and strength of a horse, and walk to Clarach.

MALCOLM PRYCE

Never ask for directions in Wales or you'll be washing spit out of your hair for a fortnight.

ROWAN ATKINSON

The journey from Carmarthen to Aberystwyth by train is one of the most reposeful stretches of railed track on earth. The railway company has a contract with the bees. They don't molest the passengers or try to scrounge free rides. The trains, in return, do not disturb the pollen.

GWYN THOMAS

From as young as I remember I always expected that good things would happen to me. And to get the good things you had to get out of Wales.

STANLEY BAKER

If Wales is as wonderful as the Wales Tourist Board says, why does everyone go to Benidorm for their holidays?

GREN JONES

THE VALLEYS

We are warm-hearted, ebullient, inquisitive, emotional, extrovert. Our blood is mixed. We are the people of the Welsh valleys. We shock the staid English.

HILDA EVANS

Be patient, you shall have it now in a minute.

JOHN EDWARDS *quoting an acquaintance's misuse of the ubiquitous 'now' in general valley speech*

The Welsh have always been partial to cheese and forecasts of doom. In my native valley, we had a patriarchal neighbour who, through mouthfuls of toasted Cheddar, gave us regular news of the world's impending end.

GWYN THOMAS

If you paint a donkey red, it will be elected in the valleys.

TRADITIONAL SAYING

In Welsh villages you will always see a curtain move as you pass.

RAY MILLAND

Straight on by here, over the tump – rise, and then slow down, because you better turn down opposite where the bus stop used to be.

JOHN EDWARDS *relaying advice given to a stranger seeking directions in a South Wales valley town*

I have heard of a posh English gent who popped into a valley pub. He asked, 'Which is the quickest way to get to Cardiff from here?' The landlord thought for a moment and replied, 'Are you walking or going by car?' The posh gent said, 'By car, of course.' The landlord responded, 'That's the quickest way.'

DAVID JANDRELL

Pontrhydyfen is the kind of grey, wet valley town that produces socialists, miners and exiles.

BRENDA MADDOX

Apart from his voice, Tom Jones will always be remembered for being the pop star whose pelvic swivel caused women of all ages to whip off their knickers and throw them at him – except for those in the Welsh valleys, where they needed to hang on to at least two pairs to keep warm.

JOHN RICHARDS

Wales is a ghastly place. Huge gangs of sinewy men roam the valleys, terrorising people with their close-harmony singing. You need half a pint of phlegm in your throat just to pronounce the place names.

BLACK ADDER III

VIOLENCE

There are more crimes in Britain now due to the huge rise in the crime rate.

NEIL KINNOCK

The Football Association have given me a pat on the back because I've taken violence off the terraces and onto the pitch.

VINNIE JONES

WALES AND THE WELSH

Mention Wales to anybody in show business and they wipe away a tear.

CY ENFIELD

Finding out that your sister is black is fine. Finding out that your sister is Welsh is another thing.

A A GILL

A Welshman will give you a wrong direction rather than tell you he doesn't know where a place is.

HILDA NICHOLAS

Wales isn't so much a country as a state of mind.

IFOR WILLIAMS

Welshmen are as cunning as buggery and as obvious as the day.

CAITLIN THOMAS

The Welsh – are they the people that write about choirs and sheep and getting blotto in the rain?

NATALIE DAICHES

The Welsh answer to a problem is nearly always to appoint a committee.

GORONWY REES

The Welsh, as a people, were born disinherited.

GWYN WILLIAMS

The ordinary women of Wales are generally short and squat, ill-favoured and nasty.

DAVID MALLET

The Welsh are a nation of male-voiced choir lovers whose only hobbies are rugby and romantic involvement with sheep.

LENNY HENRY

When I met Hillary Clinton, she told me she was quarter Welsh. I said she probably tells Polish people she's quarter Polish as well.

CHARLOTTE CHURCH

Welsh women are culturally invisible.

DEIRDRE BEDDOE

The problem of Wales is not the Welsh but rather that Welshness is seen as a problem.

DAI SMITH

The Welsh remain the only race whom you can vilify without being called a racist.

A N WILSON

Wales is a country where Sunday starts early and lasts several years.

PEG BRACKEN

There are only two kinds of people in the world: those who are Welsh and those who wish they were.

BRIAN E WOOD

The Welsh are the only nation in the world that has produced no graphic or plastic art, no architecture, no drama. They just sing and blow down wind instruments of plated silver.

EVELYN WAUGH

Every day when I wake up I thank the Lord I'm Welsh.

CERYS MATTHEWS

On Saturday night a Welshman might be completely smashed, singing rude songs and mooning at passers-by on his way home from celebrating the rugby match. On Sunday morning, on the way to chapel, he's telling his children not to pick their noses.

JOHN RICHARDS

Wales has had no great women of good repute.

ARTHUR JOHNSON

I stand ready to reject, any day of the week, the idea that you should pay more tax for the privilege of being Welsh and that you should obey more laws in order to prove you're Welsh

JOHN REDWOOD

When we address our own people, we don't beat about the green bush. Remember that old advertisement, 'Her best friend wouldn't tell her'? Well, her best friend was definitely not Welsh.

DANNIE ABSE

The Welsh can't rest until we've made sure we're all cousins.

HYWEL KERRY JONES

The Welsh, like the Irish, are impulsive. One of the charms of the Irish is that they forget you immediately your back is turned. The Welsh may also share this virtue.

H V MORTON

I am, after all, the authentic dark voice of my tortured part of the world, Wales.

RICHARD BURTON

WEATHER

When elsewhere it is summer, it is winter in Wales.

PIERRE DE LANGTOFT

There is a kind of apathy about things in Wales. The poor accept their lot and the well-to-do their comfort. And the farmers pray only for rain.

ALUN LEWIS

There's something in our weather that is hostile to treats, feasts and outings.

GWYN THOMAS

Welsh rain descends with the enthusiasm of someone breaking bad news. It comes down in a constant cataract. It runs round corners with the wind. It finds its way up your sleeves and down your neck. It sings a song on the roads as it runs to join other rivulets and form a little mountain torrent.

H V MORTON

The Welsh are just Italians in the rain.

ELAINE MORGAN

Wales is full of ugly chapels, hidden money, psalm-singing and rain.

NORMAN LEWIS

The Welsh are not meant to go out in the sun. They start to photosynthesise.

RHYS IFANS

The greatest enemy to the man who has to carry on his body all his wardrobe is rain. No seaman ever searched the heavens for a dark speck, or astronomer for a new light, as does this homeless man for a sign of it. To escape from the coming deluge, he seeks shelter in the public library, which is the only free shelter available, and there he sits for hours, staring at one page, not a word of which he has read or, for that matter, intends to read.

W H DAVIES

'Oh, Rhys,' she said, 'shut the bedroom window, will you? It's bitter cold outside.' 'All right, luv,' he replied. 'Do you think it's any warmer out there now?'

WYNFORD JONES

The London, Midland and Scottish line served a dual purpose for the people of Blaenau. The train coming along the Conwy valley entered the town through a very long tunnel. Very often, on the Saturday morning of a rainy week, my father would pack me off to the station to ask what the weather was like on the other side of the tunnel. Sometimes the reply would be, 'Tell your father it's not raining on the other side of the tunnel and it's a heat wave in Llandudno.'

AELWYN ROBERTS

WEIGHT

My beloved is as stout as a Welsh chicken.

LIZ TAYLOR *on Richard Burton in 1975*

The first time I saw myself on television I was so embarrassed I stopped eating for a week.

TERRY GRIFFITHS

My interest in athletes has been sharpened by all the talk of drugs that can alter their physical scope. I cannot now watch an eight stone girl without a whimsical conviction that she is, without chemical prompting, a fourteen stone, bearded, male fitter, shaven and shrunk for just that day.

GWYN THOMAS

I know a man who's so fat he's half-Welsh, half-English and half-Scottish.

EMRYS ELLIS

WORK

Ray Reardon once drove all the way from Wales to London to play one frame of snooker during a charity evening. He potted only one ball, bowed to the audience, then drove all the way home, because he was on shift work the next day as a policeman.

JACK KARNEHM

I can't afford friends in this town. I lose too many working days attending the funerals.

MALCOLM PRYCE *on Aberystwyth*

WRITERS AND WRITING

The sentimental view of Wales as a demi-paradise, a land of innocent country maidens and romantic squires, he killed stone dead.

JOHN ROWLANDS *on Caradoc Evans*

There are plenty of Welsh people whose prime literature is a soccer or rugby match programme.

TREVOR FISHLOCK

I couldn't write my autobiography. Too many people would be hurt by it. The only way I could do it was if I was 98 years old and I was the only person I knew left alive.

TOM JONES

It was as though some new-style yahoo had flung a bucket of dung through the Welsh parlour window, and in case anyone was genteel or well-meaning enough not to notice anything amiss, had flung the bucket in after, with a long-reverberating clangour.

GWYN JONES *on Caradoc Evans*

I've got an interesting idea for a novel: an alcoholic sheep who sings carols outside valley chapels in the rain and dreams of playing rugby for Wales.

DAFYDD LLOYD

A Welsh Tennyson would have found his audience in the small farms and the labourers' cottages, not in the drawing-rooms and studies.

WYN GRIFFITHS

Far too many people try to write the Great Novel in Welsh. What's the point, when there are no people to read it?

FFOWC ELIS

Not one Welshman has produced fiction which has lived six months after the day of its publication.

CARADOC EVANS

GENERAL SPECULATIONS

The most dangerous thing in the world is to try to leap a chasm in two jumps.

DAVID LLOYD GEORGE

We know what happens to people who stay in the middle of the road. They get knocked down.

ANEURIN BEVAN

What is culture but palaver and swank? I turn up my nose at it.

IDRIS DAVIES

There are few places in the world more forlorn than a nightclub in daylight.

MALCOLM PRYCE

A doctor can bury his mistakes, but an architect can only advise his client to plant vines.

FRANK LLOYD WRIGHT

The only things we guard with real success are the secrets of our shames.

GWYN THOMAS

A person with no bee in the bonnet is a person in the grave.

RHYS DAVIES

Isn't life a terrible thing, thank God?

DYLAN THOMAS

Welsh Wit and Wisdom is just one of a whole range of
Welsh-interest publications from Y Lolfa. For a full list of
publications, ask for your free copy of our catalogue
– or simply surf into our secure website,

www.ylolfa.com

and order online.

TALYBONT, CEREDIGION, CYMRU (WALES), SY24 5AP
email ylolfa@ylolfa.com
website www.ylolfa.com
tel. (01970) 832 304
fax 832 782